CHRISTIAN ENCOUNTERS

ANNE
BRADSTREET

CHRISTIAN ENCOUNTERS

ANNE
BRADSTREET

D. B. KELLOGG

THOMAS NELSON
Since 1798

NASHVILLE   DALLAS   MEXICO CITY   RIO DE JANEIRO

Published in Nashville, Tennessee, by Thomas Nelson. Thomas Nelson is a registered trademark of Thomas Nelson, Inc.

Thomas Nelson, Inc., titles may be purchased in bulk for educational, business, fund-raising, or sales promotional use. For information, please e-mail SpecialMarkets@ThomasNelson.com.

Scripture references are from the King James Version, unless otherwise indicated.

Library of Congress Cataloging-in-Publication Data

Kellogg, D. B.
  Anne Bradstreet / D. B. Kellogg.
     p. cm. — (Christian encounters series)
  Includes bibliographical references.
  ISBN 978-1-59555-109-2
  1. Bradstreet, Anne, 1612?–1672—Criticism and interpretation. 2. Christian poetry, American—History and criticism. I. Title.
  PS712.K45 2010
  811'.1—dc22
                                            2010006516

Printed in the United States of America

10 11 12 13 HCI 6 5 4 3 2 1

TO ALL THE WOMEN
WHO HAVE BEEN
AHEAD OF THEIR TIME

CONTENTS

INTRODUCTION

Boom! Boom! Two of the *Arbella*'s cannons announced its arrival as it sailed into the waters off Plum Cove in June 1630. The passengers from England had crowded onto the deck before 4:00 a.m. to get their first glimpses of the new land, the Massachusetts Bay Colony.[1]

At least one passenger, Anne Bradstreet, was a reluctant immigrant. She had no choice about being on that ship and crossing the Atlantic. The eighteen-year-old accompanied her husband, her parents, her siblings, and many friends as they left behind everything they had ever known. The new land was nothing like the land of her birth, a land of established institutions, towns and cities, grand churches, and houses with fine furniture and finer libraries. She later wrote that she found "a new world and new manners" with which she was much distressed, yet eventually she was "convinced it was the way of God," and she "submitted to it."[2] As she matured as a woman, her faith also matured. Her relationship with God deepened, and she firmly believed that "in Truth, it is the absence or presence of God that makes Heaven or Hell." She could see God's wondrous works in the heavens above and the earth below, the regularity of day and night, and the passing of seasons as he provided for "this great household upon the Earth."[3]

When Anne stepped onto New England soil for the first time, she was a daughter, sister, friend, and fairly new wife. Too long a time would pass, she thought, before she became a mother, but she bore eight children, and all survived to adulthood.

Throughout the drama of establishing the Massachusetts Bay Colony, men were the leading characters, not the least of whom were Anne's father, Thomas Dudley, and her husband, Simon Bradstreet; and women were the supporting cast. A woman's pursuit of a role as anything other than a good Christian, wife, and mother was unseemly at best and heretical at worst, and Anne was aware that people would object to her as a writer: "I am obnoxious to each carping tongue / Who says my hand a needle better fits" than a "Poet's pen." She heeded the lessons of her mother about how to be a good Puritan woman, but she was inspired by another woman from an earlier century, Queen Elizabeth I. In her "happy reign," wrote Anne, "Who was so good, so just, so learned, so wise / From all the Kings on earth she won the prize." She "wiped off the aspersion of her Sex, / That women wisdom lack to play the Rex [ruler]."[4] Anne had the wisdom, determination, and ability to play the poet.

Historian Samuel Eliot Morison wrote, "There was one person in early Massachusetts who wrote poetry for poetry's sake, or merely to express her own thoughts and aspirations, with no hope or expectation of an audience beyond her family and friends,"[5] and he was talking about Anne Bradstreet. She revealed her heart in poems about her beloved husband, children, grandchildren, and parents. She relied on her fine intellect and years of study to craft lengthy poems about history, science, and philosophy. She reflected on her God, her inner struggles, and her extreme physical challenges in her "Meditations."

Her book of poetry, *The Tenth Muse Lately Sprung Up in America*, was published in England in 1650, not by Anne but by her brother-in-law, and possibly without Anne's knowledge. It was popular throughout the seventeenth century and into the eighteenth century, but gradually her poetic work was pushed onto lower bookshelves, where it gathered dust and was overlooked. Then John Harvard Ellis reprinted *The Tenth Muse Lately Sprung Up in America* in 1867, and poet Conrad Aiken included some of her poems in his 1929 anthology of American poetry and "initiated a serious revaluation" of Anne.[6] John Berryman's poem "Homage to Mistress Bradstreet" in 1953 and the feminist movement, beginning in earnest in the mid-1960s, introduced an even more "serious revaluation" of her work. Poet Adrienne Rich applauded Anne by writing that the "texture [of her work] is essentially both Puritan and feminine. . . . Her individualism lies in her choice of material rather than in her style. . . . To have written poems, the first good poems in America, while rearing eight children, lying frequently sick, keeping house at the edge of the wilderness, was to have managed a poet's range and extension within confines as severe as any American poet has confronted."[7] Samuel Eliot Morison pointed out that Anne was "unusual . . . among the men and women of the first generation [of the settlers of New England] in that her character, her thoughts, and her religion were expressed in poetry that has endured, and will endure."[8] The reluctant immigrant, Anne Bradstreet, became a reluctant historical figure when she stepped into history and literature books as the "first woman poet to be published in colonial America."[9]

ENGLAND

Anne's story begins in Northampton, in the central part of England about sixty miles northwest of London as the crow flies. Born there in 1612, Anne was the second child of Thomas and Dorothy Dudley. They already had four-year-old Samuel, who was to remain their only son. Thomas and Dorothy had married in 1603, the year of Queen Elizabeth's death.

Anne's mother, Dorothy Yorke, was born in 1582 in the county of Northamptonshire; she was "a gentlewoman both of good estate and good extraction."[1] Dorothy's father was Edmund Yorke, a yeoman.[2] At that time, a yeoman was a landowner who worked the land, with or without laborers, depending on his wealth. He was a member of what was regarded as the middle class.

Thomas Dudley was born in October of 1576 in Yardley Hastings near Northampton to Captain Roger Dudley and his wife, Susanna, née Thorne. Genealogists and historians still debate Roger's connection to the poet Sir Philip Sidney and to the Sutton-Dudleys of Dudley Castle in Worcestershire, but Thomas seemed sure of the connection. Through his maternal side of the family, Thomas was a descendant of Henry II of England. Thomas was just a boy when his father was killed in battle, fighting for Queen Elizabeth I, and he was an early teen when his mother died. Family friends provided a home for the orphan, who had been left £500 in trust. They made certain that the young man received a good education, and eventually he became a page for a family of nobility in Northampton. Having a position as a page was no small thing then; he was not like a menial servant. Among other tasks, he learned how to oversee an estate.

With Queen Elizabeth I on the throne, the nation rose to a powerful position in the world, and her policies united the country. She said, "Be ye ensured that I will be as good unto you as ever a Queen was to her People,"[3] and she meant it. She did not let her people down. The economy flourished. The queen's forty-five-year reign was a golden age of overseas expansion and trade, literature and the arts, and scientific thought. Navigator and historian Sir Walter Raleigh, explorer Sir Francis Drake, philosopher Francis Bacon, mathematician and physicist Sir Isaac Newton, poets Sir Philip Sidney and Edmund Spenser, and playwrights William Shakespeare, Christopher Marlowe, and Ben Jonson thrived. Queen Elizabeth reinstated the Church of England (the Anglican Church) as the state religion and confirmed Protestant doctrine with the Act of Supremacy and the Act of Uniformity, but she did not declare war against her Catholic subjects. All of her accomplishments are even more remarkable given the state of the nation she inherited, which was in dire financial straits and suffered religious turmoil between Catholics and Protestants.

Queen Elizabeth I commissioned Thomas Dudley, then age twenty or twenty-one, as a captain to command eighty volunteers from Northampton. They joined the forces of Henry IV of France against Philip II of Spain and participated in the six-month siege of Amiens in 1597. Henry's forces succeeded in regaining the city from the Spaniards. Dudley and his volunteers did not actually fight while in France, but they gained experience as soldiers in the field.[4]

Upon his return from France, Dudley became a clerk for his mother's kinsman Judge Nicholls[5] in Northampton. Nicholls was considered a fair judge and a man of integrity. In addition to learning law from him, Dudley accompanied the judge to London for court-related matters, and there he witnessed some of the best legal minds in the land at work. The lessons in law and justice paid off in Dudley's future in unanticipated ways for him, his family, and his country. He worked for Nicholls until the judge's death.[6]

By 1620, the Dudleys moved north to Sempringham when forty-four-year-old Thomas became the steward of Theophilus Clinton, the fourth Earl of Lincoln. Educated at Cambridge, the nineteen-year-old earl had inherited the family estates, along with substantial debts of about £20,000 that dated back to his grandfather's profligate days. He did not have the skills to oversee the estates by himself, and men who had been hired to help him achieve a sound financial position had failed miserably. Dudley was recommended as a trustworthy man with the business acumen to guide the earl out of his debt. Never one to be deterred by a challenge, Dudley went to work and saw to it that the earl was not only free of debt but also making a substantial profit each year. It was said that the grateful earl did no "business of moment without Mr. Dudley's counsel."[7]

Sempringham proved to be a wonderful place for the Dudley children to grow up. Samuel and Anne welcomed two sisters, Patience and Sarah, before the move, and Mercy joined the family within a year of the move.[8] As the eldest sister, Anne helped her mother with the young ones, and she took that duty seriously. But dozens of servants took care of most tasks in the upper-class surroundings of the earl's home. The children were well acquainted with the earl's family members who lived on the main estate or nearby: the earl's mother, Elizabeth; his wife, Bridget, the Countess of Lincoln, whom he married in 1622; his children; and his siblings Lady Arbella and Lady Susan, among others. (The earl had at least nine brothers and sisters.) Even if the Dudley children were not active participants in the family's entertaining, sometimes with dancing and music, they watched the goings-on. From the nobles they learned fine manners that complemented what they learned from their mother.

For Anne, having access to the earl's library was a delightful part of her years on the estate. Although their father did not neglect the education of any of his children, he took special interest in that of Anne. They shared a love of books that was atypical for a father and a daughter, especially in that era—a favorite was Sir Walter Raleigh's *History of the World*—and that bond remained strong until the end of each one's life. Anne seemed taken with poetry, especially poems by Guillame de Salluste Du Bartas, a Frenchman. Like most Puritan girls and women, Anne was taught to read so that she could better understand the Scriptures and eventually teach them to her young children before they could read. Not all Puritan females were taught to write, however. Anne learned to do both well, and existing copies of her handwriting show a firm, clear hand.

The English Scriptures influenced both the daily life and the language of the English people. Although it was not the first Bible to be translated into English, the Geneva Bible of 1560, dedicated to Queen Elizabeth I, was the first Bible to number the verses, and it also had helpful marginal notes, which contributed to the Bible's popularity.[9] Shakespeare read it, and the translators of the King James Bible used it as a source. Queen Elizabeth's successor, King James I, commissioned the new version at the behest of a large number of English ministers, and in 1611, the year before Anne's birth, the King James Version appeared. Here is an example of the two versions for Psalm 46:1:[10]

GENEVA BIBLE
God is our hope and strength,
and help in troubles,
ready to be found.

KING JAMES VERSION
God is our refuge and strength,
a very present help in trouble.

And here is Genesis 3:7:

GENEVA BIBLE
They sewed fig leaves together
and made themselves breeches.

KING JAMES VERSION
They sewed fig leaves together,
and made themselves aprons.

Anne and her family had both the King James and the Geneva versions, and they used them in discussions of and meditations on Scripture. Thomas and Dorothy Dudley established a pattern of daily prayers for the family, and Thomas read psalms aloud and talked about the sermons they heard at church.[11] Anne clearly was paying attention to what she heard in church from the minister and to the devotions at home led by her father, and she took the lessons to heart, even as a youngster. Years later she wrote that she became aware of her sinful ways at age six or seven. She did her best to avoid lying and disobeying her parents, but she was not always successful. She was troubled when she felt overtaken with such evils, and she could not rest until she confessed all in prayer to God. She was also "troubled at the neglect of Private Duties [meditating and praying in private]," and she felt she was "too often tardy that way." Reading Scriptures, however, comforted her, and the more she understood, the more solace she found in them.[12]

Reared as faithful members of the Church of England, the Dudley family gradually embraced Puritanism. Many Puritans who fled England with the rise of the Catholic Queen Mary had returned when Queen Elizabeth ascended the throne. While in Northampton, Dudley had become fond of certain ministers, and he was leaning toward their Puritan beliefs. At the time of son Samuel's birth, Thomas and Dorothy attended All Saints Church, but in Sempringham they were surrounded by Puritanism.[13] Many "learned and able Puritan ministers, busily engaged in stirring the hearts of people with political and religious principles," lived and preached in the nearby town of Boston (also in Lincolnshire). With their growing influence on him, Dudley became a "zealous asserter"[14] of Puritanism, and Anne felt that influence too.

A brief history lesson on Puritanism is in order here. Perhaps the most concise definition of *Puritanism* comes from the illustrious and plain-speaking historian Samuel Eliot Morison, who wrote, "Puritanism was a way of life based on the belief that the Bible was the word of God, and the whole word of God. Puritans were the Englishmen who endeavored to live according to that light." The term came to refer to English Protestants who "wished to carry out the Reformation to its logical conclusion, and purge the Anglican Church of forms and ceremonies for which there was no warrant in the Bible." Puritanism had both religious and moral aspects.[15]

King Henry VIII was responsible for making Anglicanism, instead of Catholicism, the state church of England in 1534, and within twenty years, English Puritanism gained a foothold. The Puritans considered Anglican clergy poorly educated and unskilled at preaching. Puritans opposed kneeling at Communion, exchanging rings in marriage, and having a cross in church because all those signs reflected Catholicism. As far as the Puritans were concerned, baptism and Communion were the only two biblical sacraments.

Puritanism did not equal Calvinism,[16] but they shared similar doctrinal points:

Total depravity (humanity's utter corruption since the Fall)
Unconditional election (the idea that God had decreed who was damned and who was saved from before the beginning of the world)
Limited atonement (the idea that Christ died for the elect only)
Irresistible grace (regeneration as entirely a work of God,

which cannot be resisted and to which the sinner
contributes nothing)

Perseverance of the saints (the elect, despite their
backsliding and faintness of heart, cannot fall away
from grace)[17]

Around 1624, Thomas Dudley left his job as steward for
the Earl of Lincoln and moved the family to Boston. There
they worshipped at St. Botolph's, where the pastor was John
Cotton. St. Botolph's was (and is) a very large, impressive
church built from 1309 to 1390. A Puritan leader who looked
up to John Calvin, Cotton had attended Emmanuel College
at Cambridge University. Emmanuel College has been called
a "nursery of Puritanism" because many of the "staunchest"
early Puritans attended there or were taught by its graduates.[18]
Cotton learned his lessons well, not the least of which was
an extensive knowledge of Hebrew, and he was a compelling
speaker. His friendship with the Dudley family soon had an
important bearing on Anne's future.

The timing is somewhat murky about when Thomas
Dudley returned to his job as steward for the Earl of Lincoln.
It is certain that in 1626 the earl was imprisoned in the Tower
of London for opposing a "loan" demanded by King Charles I,
who had succeeded James I in 1625. Charles I was no friend of
the Puritans, and the earl was no friend of the king.[19]

The Dudleys were definitely back in Sempringham with
the earl by 1628 because Anne was stricken with smallpox that
year and she was treated on the estate. Her health from childhood was never robust, and she experienced various serious

illnesses throughout her life. Her constant prayer to God was to set her free from her afflictions. As a young child, she had had a fever that confined her to bed for some time, and even then she was given to introspection about her faith.[20] As an adult, Anne recalled the events of that episode and wrote:

> My burning flesh in sweat did boil,
> My aching head did break;
> From side to side for ease I toil,
> So faint I could not speak.
> . . . .
> O, heal my Soul, thou know'st I said,
> Though flesh consume to naught;
> What though in dust it shall be laid,
> To glory it shall be brought.
> Thou heard, thy rod thou did remove,
> And spared my Body frail. . . .
> O, Praises to my mighty God,
> Praise to my Lord, I say,
> Who hath redeemed my Soul from [the] pit.[21]

A fever accompanied the smallpox that overtook her, and after she recovered, Anne praised God for saving her, although it was apparently a close call. The deadly disease had no cure or means of prevention in the 1600s, and the treatment provided little, if any, relief and probably contributed even more to the sufferer's weakness.

When Anne complained of slight fever accompanied by a headache (or backache), her parents were concerned. But when a rash appeared a few days later and her fever spiked, their concern grew to alarm because they knew that she had smallpox. She was confined to bed, covered with blankets, and placed near a fire. The room was kept dark. Instead of water to drink, she was given hot ale or a mixture of bitter herbs. In addition to having painful skin eruptions that could result in scarring, Anne's internal organs could have been damaged. Severe cases of smallpox resulted in blindness and even death caused by toxemia or hemorrhaging; sometimes secondary infections killed the sufferer. The usual course of the disease was run within two weeks.[22] Of course, the recovery time depended on the individual, and Anne's recovery was prolonged.

No painting exists to show us what Anne looked like, but her face must not have been scarred by the lesions. A relative wrote, "There needs no painting to that comely face, / That in its native beauty hath such grace."[23]

While she was recovering, she had plenty of time to think, and years later Anne wrote that "the Lord laid his hand sore upon me" with the smallpox, and she "confessed [her] Pride and Vanity" to him. She was grateful to the Lord for restoring her, but she believed that she "rendered not to him according to the benefit received."[24]

Anne felt the need to confess more to God. The stirrings began when she was "about fourteen or fifteen," she wrote, and she found her "heart more carnal and sitting loose from God," and "vanity and the follies of youth" taking hold of her.[25] The stirrings most likely had to do with the handsome young man Simon Bradstreet, who was nine years older than she and worked on the Sempringham estate with her father. Whether it was his kindness, his intelligence, or his good looks—or all three—she was smitten with him. And at some point he was taken with her.

Simon came to the estate in 1622 after he had been at Emmanuel College following his father's death; he eventually earned a BA and an MA at that college. Rev. John Cotton knew both the Bradstreet and the Dudley families, and he discussed the young man's future with Thomas Dudley.[26] Glad to have someone to help him and pleased by Simon's upbringing and education, Dudley agreed to train Bradstreet as an assistant steward.

Portraits survive of Bradstreet as an older man, and he has been described as having a "broad, benignant forehead," "clear, dark eyes," and a "firm, well-cut nose."[27] His father was from a wealthy family in Suffolk, and he, too, attended Emmanuel College. When Simon was born, the elder Bradstreet was a Nonconformist minister (meaning he did not conform to the ceremonies of the Church of England) at Horbling in Lincolnshire, and Simon attended grammar school there.

Simon performed the duties of the earl's steward in Dudley's absence while he and the family were in Boston. When the Dudleys returned to Sempringham, Simon assumed a new position as steward to the Countess of Warwick. The countess was the former Susan Rowe, whose father had been Lord Mayor of London and whose first husband had been an alderman in London. Her second husband was Robert Rich, the second Earl of Warwick, a Puritan who briefly attended Emmanuel College and had extensive trade and colonizing interests in the New World. Like the Earl of Lincoln, the Earl of Warwick refused to pay the "loan" demanded by King Charles I. Since her husband was often away, the countess needed someone like Simon on-site to tend to daily affairs. The earl's family had two residences: Leighs (or Leez) Priory, a country estate in Chelmsford (about forty miles northeast of London) in Essex County; and Warwick House near London.[28]

Anne was only ten and Simon, nineteen, when they first met, so Simon regarded her as just a young friend, one of the children of his mentor, Dudley. The courtship probably developed about the time Anne started having her stirrings, but Anne and Simon's relationship was unusual compared to that of most young Puritan couples because they had shared the same roof for several years while living on the earl's estate. They saw each other regularly, and he often ate with the Dudley family. Each learned about the other's strengths and weaknesses; favorite sermons, scriptures, books, and more.

After Simon began work for the Earl of Warwick, seeing Anne was more difficult because of the distance separating them, but the bond between the two was already formed by then. Despite their age difference, there is every indication that Simon had only respect for Anne's intellect and opinions. His love for her is evident in their forty-four-year love story that defies modern mistaken views of Puritans and their attitudes toward marital life.

When he decided to ask the Dudleys for Anne's hand, Simon did not have to work hard to convince them that he would be a good husband for their daughter. They already knew him well and trusted him. The couple married in 1628, even though the sixteen-year-old bride was not yet fully recovered from the aftereffects of smallpox. They lived on the country estate of the countess and looked forward to what the future would bring them. Neither one could have envisioned how far they would go together and how far-reaching their influence would be felt.

AN UNEXPECTED
NEW VENTURE

Anne and Simon Bradstreet settled into a comfortable routine of newlyweds on their own, and their domestic tranquility was troubled only by the fact that Anne was not yet expecting. Simon was doing well on his job, and Anne was learning to become mistress of her home. By 1630, eighteen-year-old Anne was increasingly distressed that she did not have a child or one on the way. Then in that year, troubles brewing on the political and religious fronts demanded the couple's immediate attention and forced them to make a life-changing decision.

A group of Puritans planned to leave England and settle in the Massachusetts Bay Colony. The Dudleys and the rest of their children were among them; the decision had been made even before Anne's marriage two years earlier. Simon was uncertain that leaving was a wise move for him and Anne, but the thoughtful man considered the pros and cons. The couple prayed together about it. Undoubtedly Simon talked over the situation with his wife, his father-in-law, and his many friends. Anne was torn: she had no desire to be a pioneer in the wilderness, but she feared that she would not see her parents and siblings again if she and Simon remained in England. When Simon came to believe that severe persecution of Puritans was imminent, he saw that they had no viable alternative. They would join the migration to the Massachusetts Bay Colony.

King Charles I made it plain that he opposed the Puritans. He dissolved Parliament in 1629, where many members supported Puritanism, and did not call it again until 1640. The Puritans had valid concerns that he would reintroduce elements of Catholicism into the English church. The king was a proponent of High Anglican worship, and his wife, Henrietta Maria, was the daughter of the French king Henry IV. (Henry had been raised as a Huguenot, meaning a Calvinist, but upon reaching the throne, he had to renounce that faith and receive instruction in Catholicism.) Bishop William Laud was King Charles's man in the Anglican Church who wanted the return of church lands that had been taken during the Reformation, and he insisted on a strict Anglican ritual, much to the dismay of Puritans.

By the time the king and Laud had finished with their campaign against Puritans, they had imprisoned some Puritans and taken positions away from others. Puritan clergymen were particular targets, and before 1630, at least three hundred lost their posts—more lost them later.[1] Samuel Eliot Morison believed that if King Charles I and Bishop Laud "had not attempted religious innovations in the direction of Rome, if they had respected the ritual and doctrine of the Church as Elizabeth . . . had left them, the puritans [*sic*] might never have become associated with radicalism and democracy."[2] And they might never have established the Massachusetts Bay Colony.

According to theologian J. I. Packer, the name of Puritan had been a "satirical smear word implying peevishness, censoriousness, conceit, and a measure of hypocrisy" beyond the meaning related to the church since the 1560s. Packer believed that a more accurate description of Puritans was that they were "sober, conscientious, and cultured citizens, persons of principle, determined and disciplined. . . . Spiritual warfare made the Puritans what they were" because the Puritans lost, more or less, "every public battle." Packer commended the Puritans for the "quality of their spiritual experience," "passion for effective action," "family stability," "sense of human worth," and the "ideal of church renewal." They also continually sought to hear God's voice.[3]

The Puritans who joined the Great Migration (1630–40) to New England came from all forty English counties, but more were from East Anglian counties, including Lincolnshire, than any other area. A quick scan of the counties in present-day Massachusetts reveals that the state shares names with the counties of Norfolk, Suffolk, and Essex, and the city name Boston.[4]

Augustine Jones, a biographer of Thomas Dudley, wrote that the doctrine of liberty "took a deep and permanent hold of the minds of the people who inhabited that region of country north of London on the eastern side of England, including Lincolnshire." From the time of the Reformation, that part of England had been inhabited by "bold, independent, thoughtful, and industrious citizens."[5] A study done almost three hundred years later found that East Anglia produced the "greatest statesmen, scientists, ecclesiastics, scholars, and artists in English history" of all English regions.[6]

Most immigrants to New England were country squires and yeomen who were "thrifty and prosperous in their old homes from which their devotion to an idea made them voluntary exiles," observed historian John Fiske. "In all history there has been no other instance of colonization so exclusively effected by picked and chosen men."[7] English historian John R. Green explained the Massachussetts colonists:

> [They] were not, like the earlier colonists of the South, "broken men," adventurers, bankrupts, criminals, or simply poor men and artisans like the Pilgrim Fathers of the *Mayflower*. They were, in great part, men of the professional and middle classes; some of them men of large landed estate, some zealous clergymen, some shrewd London lawyers or young scholars from Oxford. The bulk were God-fearing farmers from Lincolnshire and the eastern counties.[8]

Within two years of the accession of Charles I, some well-to-do Puritans in Lincolnshire, including Thomas Dudley, entertained the idea of planting the gospel in New England.[9] They also contacted men in London and the western part of England about joining them. The planners were willing to invest their money in the venture, and many were willing to make the personal commitment of uprooting their families and taking them to settle the colony. The major investor, Isaac Johnson, was a wealthy landowner married to the beautiful Lady Arbella, sister of the Earl of Lincoln.[10]

These men of common sense, business sense, and firm convictions set out a methodical, legal process for bringing the idea to fruition. In 1629, they obtained a charter from the government of King Charles for the area that became the Massachusetts Bay Colony. In essence it was a joint stock corporation with a governor, deputy governor, and assistants (operating like a president and board of directors) elected by the stockholders (freemen). These men constituted the General Court. They took the charter for the colony with them, a fully legal move according to the document's terms, and having the document with them across the Atlantic kept the king's hands off it. They did not want the king to gain possession of it or to amend it to suit his ends. They knew that King James was able to confiscate the charter of Virginia in 1624 because it had remained in London, and he made it a Crown colony rather than a private colony administered by the Virginia Company. They were not about to have his successor, King Charles, do something similar to them. Early on, they made a point that hereditary government and a manorial system were not to be transported to the New World.[11]

John Winthrop was elected governor, and the deputy governor was John Humphrey (sometimes spelled Humfrey), the husband of Lady Susan, another sister of the Earl of Lincoln. Winthrop, born in 1588, was from Suffolk County. He attended Trinity College, Cambridge, and he had practiced law and been a justice of the peace. He was a devout Puritan said to be ambitious for public service. His late father had left him well off, and his first wife added to his coffers. In 1629, he lost his post in the Court of Wards and Liveries as a result of the king's policies against Puritans. Unlike most of the others in the founding group, he was not able to take his wife, Margaret, with him to New England in the early days of the settlement. Margaret was expecting a child, and she and most of their children, including the new addition to the family, were to come later.[12]

Winthrop and the others devised a multiple-step approach to settlement. First, in 1628, they sent John Endicott, a soldier by profession, to Salem to prepare the area for the colonists. His job was to build places to live, establish a church, prepare the land for crops, and so forth; he served as temporary governor until 1630. Second, in 1629 they sent ships carrying about three hundred people, including workmen, and a number of cows, goats, and horses.[13] Third, ships bearing a greater number of people and abundant supplies were to set out in 1630. Anne and Simon and the Dudley family were to be on the lead ship of the 1630 expedition. Knowing about these preliminary efforts was small comfort to Anne, but she understood that at least she and Simon would have a place to live when they got to the colony.

These Puritans, relying on God and constantly seeking his guidance, were going to shape a new life in New England. One historian stated, "They might have stayed [in England] and defied persecution with less trouble than it cost them to cross the ocean and found a new state,"[14] but that was not the way of these determined people. Most, like Anne, never returned to England.

"WE SHALL BE AS A CITY UPON A HILL"

The ship had been the *Eagle*, but it was rechristened the *Arbella* in honor of its noblest passenger, Lady Arbella. Commanded by Captain Peter Melbourne (sometimes spelled Milbourne), it had twenty-eight guns and a crew of fifty or more. It was to be the flagship because it was a larger-than-average vessel for its time, capable of carrying between 350 and 400 tons. Three other ships, the *Talbot*, the *Ambrose*, and the *Jewel*, would be in the group leaving in the spring of 1630 for New England. Seven others would follow later, one of which was the already famous *Mayflower*.[1] Anne and Simon, Anne's parents and her siblings, ranging in age from twenty-two to nine, Governor John Winthrop with two of his sons, Sir Richard Saltonstall with three sons and two daughters, Rev. George Philips and his wife, William Coddington and his wife, and seven or eight other passengers would join Lady Arbella and her husband on the *Arbella* as they sailed from Southampton.[2]

To prepare for the voyage, Anne had to decide what to take and what to leave behind. There was limited space on the ship, and she could pack only essential clothing, bedding, a few precious books, food, and basic necessities to set up housekeeping. Later on, when ships were regularly going back and forth from the colony to England, they would send for most of their furniture and order more clothing and household items.

After saying good-bye to friends and family, the Dudleys, the Bradstreets, and the Johnsons took a ship from Lincolnshire to Southampton so that they could board the *Arbella* to cross the Atlantic. That was much easier on them and faster than bumping and bouncing three hundred miles overland in coaches on poor roads. Southampton was then and remains a major port city on the south coast about sixty miles southwest of London.

While they were still in British waters, an unexpected honor befell fifty-four-year-old Thomas Dudley. Although John Humphrey was the duly elected deputy governor, his business affairs did not permit him to leave England at that time.[3] Dudley was elected in his place.

Rev. John Cotton, the longtime friend of the Dudleys and Bradstreets, came aboard the *Arbella*, which was docked in Southampton, to deliver a farewell sermon. The sermon of about five thousand words was intended to send the passengers on their way with a positive spirit, knowing that God blessed their enterprise. To support his statements, Cotton quoted from the Old and New Testaments, and he even cited Greek terms. It is a good example of a Puritan sermon, relying heavily on the Bible.

The opening verse was 2 Samuel 7:10: "Moreover I will appoint a place for my people Israel, and will plant them, that they may dwell in a place of their own, and move no more." Cotton emphasized that the verse applied to his listeners that day because they would have a place of their own where they would dwell like "Free-holders" and the "sonnes of wickednesse shall afflict them no more."[4] Going further, he stated that when a colony was planted by a group going together, as they were, God would bless and prosper it as he had done in Philippi (see Acts 16:12).

God is our Landlord, and the earth is his, was Cotton's view. As the apostles discovered, the Lord's people may have to flee from evil, avoid persecution, and go to another place appointed by God (Acts 13:46–47). Not only were the Puritans to offer themselves to God's service in that place, but they must make sure that their children served God too. God is also a Gardener, and when he promised to plant a people, "their dayes shall be as the dayes of a Tree" (see Isaiah 65:22). However, if they rebelled against the God who planted them, he would root them out: one way to abide by God's Word was to be sure that it was "ingrafted" into them.[5]

Cotton urged the travelers not to forget those left in England. He also encouraged them, as they settled the new land, to work with the Native Americans so that they could "make them partakers of [their] precious faith." They should look out for others in their midst and be public spirited: "This care of universall helpfulness was the prosperity of the first Plantation of the Primitive Church."[6] They should always keep in their hearts and live by the words of Acts 4:32: "The multitude of them that believed were of one heart and of one soul: neither said any of them that ought of the things which he possessed was his own: but they had all things common."

Cotton ended by praying, "Neglect not walls, and bul-warkes, and fortifications for your owne defence; but ever let the Name of the Lord be your strong Tower; and the word of his Promise the Rocke of your Refuge. His word that made heaven and earth will not faile, till heaven and earth be no more. Amen."[7]

With faith, hope, and intense prayers, the passengers of the *Arbella* set sail from Southampton on March 22. They were on their way! They reached the Isle of Wight a few days later, a distance of about thirty miles, on Easter. At Yarmouth, on the northwestern tip of the Isle of Wight, they were becalmed. They were *not* on their way! The winds were just not strong enough to fill the ship's sails.[8]

Many women, including Lady Arbella and Anne and her mother and probably her sisters, went on shore to take a break from life on the ship and breathe fresh air unlike what they found belowdecks. Just having solid ground under her feet for a little while longer must have lifted Anne's spirits.

At last they were able to leave the channel on April 8, and they had a relatively uneventful day. The next day was a differ-ent story. Crewmen spotted eight ships on the horizon and called out to alert the captain. They feared the ships were carrying ene-mies or privateers (Dunkirkers). War was still ongoing between England and Spain, and conditions between England and France remained tense, although the Treaty of Susa on April 24, 1629, had supposedly ended the war between the two.[9] While at Yarmouth, Captain Melbourne had learned that at least ten privateers might be waiting for the four ships bearing the Puritans.

The captain ordered the decks cleared and preparations made for a fight. All of the men armed themselves while the women and children hurried belowdecks to ensure they would be as safe as they could be. No one was under the illusion that anywhere was safe on a ship during a battle at sea. The crew threw overboard items that could catch fire, including most of the precious bed linens, blankets, rugs, and other textiles. Anne and the other women who had so carefully packed those goods did not have time to mourn their loss.

Aware of the extreme danger facing the ship, the Puritans earnestly prayed together. The seamen likely did not join in because they were so busy and because they shared few, if any, of the passengers' religious beliefs. According to Winthrop, all of the women and children were as fearless as the men, trusting in Providence. The hurried preparations proved to be for naught; the ships were friendly. But throughout the voyage, the threat of privateers or other enemies was real. Anytime a ship was sighted in the distance, Anne must have recalled this day's events and hoped that it was another false alarm or that they could escape without harm.

She and the other passengers could not escape seasickness, storms, or quarrelsome crew members who fought each other. So many passengers were seasick early in the voyage that groans were familiar sounds throughout the ship. The smells of animals below and people regularly losing the contents of their stomachs added to the misery of all on board. After one severe storm ended, the sailors strung a rope on deck so that passengers could come up, hold on, and get fresh air and a bit of exercise to make them feel better. Feeling better was a relative term, however. The cold and the damp were unrelenting, and the loss of the blankets early in the voyage meant that they had little with which to keep themselves warm. Anne, who was not strong to begin with, must have suffered doubly in these conditions. Cases of scurvy, caused by a diet deficient in vitamin C, affected crewmen and passengers toward the end of the trip.

Getting proper nutrition was a challenge, whether in good weather or bad. Fires for cooking were built in boxes on the open deck. If the weather was stormy, no fires could be built because of the rain, and if the seas were rough, fires were not permitted because of the danger of fire spreading throughout the wooden ship. Each passenger received a ration of food, and each family or group then figured out what to do with it.[10] Some families, such as the Dudleys, Bradstreets, Winthrops, and Johnsons, had servants who did the cooking for them. More often than not, everyone had cold food, and they had to resort to dried meat. One consolation was the beer. In the hold were forty-two tuns of beer, which is about ten thousand gallons. (That is not a misspelling; a tun was a measure of capacity, about 252 gallons.)[11] Keeping water fresh for a long journey was impossible, and beer was a safe alternative. The alcohol kept algae or bacteria from contaminating the drink. Contrary to popular belief, Puritans as a whole were not teetotalers, although some were. The problem with alcohol as they saw it was overindulgence; moderation was the key in everything.

All was not misery on the voyage. The children played games during nice weather. Anne and the other women did their needlework. One day the ship passed through a large school of cod, and the sailors hauled in more than sixty fish in two hours. Whether it is a fish story or the truth, Governor Winthrop stated that some were more than forty-eight inches long.

When sea conditions were favorable, some passengers were lowered into skiffs and rowed over to other ships to pay visits and have dinner with friends; sometimes the *Arbella*'s passengers switched roles and hosted their friends. Several women, including Anne and her mother, the reverend's wife, and the Saltonstall daughters, dined with Lady Arbella in the "great cabin," which was not great in size or appointments, but it was the best the ship had to offer.

On June 1, after almost two months at sea, the *Arbella* shot off a cannon, frightening passengers who were unaware of the reason for the blast. A woman on the *Arbella* had gone into labor, and the captain was trying to get the attention of the *Jewel* sailing far ahead of them. He knew that a midwife was on the other ship. When the *Jewel*'s captain heard the cannon and saw that the *Arbella* had lowered its topsails as a sign that there was an emergency, he slowed his ship until the *Arbella* could catch up. Captain Melbourne sent over a skiff for the midwife, and she boarded the *Arbella* and safely delivered the baby.[12] The birth of a child on a voyage was not unusual, but the survival rate of the newborns was poor. A few days after this incident, another woman delivered a stillborn child.

Just as they had done at home in England, the passengers had daily prayers in the morning and the evening, and the Reverend Philips preached two sermons on Sunday. They also read or studied their Bibles and discussed what they were reading. Anne's brother, Samuel, had graduated from Emmanuel College in 1626, and he could have assisted with the study.[13]

John Winthrop spent much of his time working on a significant six-thousand-word sermon, "A Model of Christian Charity," which he delivered while the *Arbella* was still at sea. In it, he presented the work that lay before the group. He repeated words that they had often heard in their churches: man is to manifest the glory of God, promote brotherly love, and uphold justice and extend mercy. He reminded them to love their enemies and "pray for them which despitefully use you, and persecute you" (Matt. 5:44). He urged his hearers, members of the body of Christ, to look to the Lord in everything. They were in covenant with God. A less common topic, related to financial dealings, was pertinent to their new venture, and he brought up lending rules and just ways to deal with debt.

Then he offered the words that are repeated today: "We must consider that we shall be as a city upon a hill. The eyes of all people are upon us. So that if we shall deal falsely with our God in this work we have undertaken, and so cause Him to withdraw His present help from us, we shall be made a story and a by-word through the world." He warned that if they did not obey God, "we shall surely perish out of the good land whither we pass over this vast sea to possess it." He encouraged them, "Let us choose life" and cleave to God, "our life and our prosperity."[14]

Less than ten years after the Pilgrims aboard the *Mayflower* dropped anchor off Cape Cod in November 1620, the Puritans aboard the *Arbella* dropped anchor on June 12, 1630, in Plum Cove, about three miles from Salem.[15] They were more than ready to land and create their "city upon a hill" with God's help.

Even though she heard and understood Winthrop's words, Anne Bradstreet had a heavy heart about what her future held in the colony. She was overwhelmed. In her surviving prose and poetry, her only comment about these early days was that when she came to New England, "I found a new world and new manners, at which my heart rose [in protest]."[16]

NEW ENGLAND

They had been at sea seventy-two days. All things considered, the voyage was fairly uneventful, given what happened to ships that arrived later or made the return trip to England. For that Anne was thankful.

Governor John Winthrop wrote that "a smell of the shore, like the smell of a garden," wafted through the air and was the first thing to greet them. It must have seemed like heaven after the smells of the ship. Next arrived John Endicott, the temporary governor, and Winthrop took over as the official governor from him. Samuel Skelton, the former vicar of Sempringham, had been in the colony since 1629 and had become the pastor of the church in Salem. He too greeted the new arrivals.[1]

Later in the day Winthrop and the other men of the General Court and a few women were rowed in skiffs to Salem, where they had a meal of venison and beer. Most of the passengers went to the nearby shore of Cape Ann and found and ate wild strawberries.[2] Anne and her siblings were probably among the strawberry-gathering group. They all returned to the ship to spend the next two days and nights.[3]

By June 14, the *Arbella* anchored in Salem harbor. Over the next few weeks, the remaining ships commissioned by the group arrived. By summer's end, the population had increased by about one thousand people.[4] Whether early or late arrivals, all were subject to the same privations of the colony.

As Anne and Simon prepared to leave the ship and oversee the unloading of their belongings, they were shocked to learn that they had no place to put those belongings. Before they left England, they understood that a house would be ready for them, but like many others on their ship, they would have to share living quarters for an undefined period. Even worse, food was in short supply. About eighty people who had been sent over with John Endicott died during the winter of 1629–30. The survivors were either so ill or in such poor condition because of lack of food that they could not plant or gather crops or build the needed number of dwellings. Even when the other ships arrived, the news was not much better because many provisions had spoiled or had been mistakenly left behind, with one ship's captain thinking the other had loaded the goods.[5] It was a case of each side depending on the other for food, but neither side could fulfill the need. As soon as they could, they sent one ship to England with the mission of bringing back food.

Winthrop and the other leaders contemplated the best course of action. They were dissatisfied with conditions in Salem, although eventually they had their goods unloaded there. They decided to reload everything (no small endeavor in itself) and take their goods to Charlestown, down the Charles and Mystic

Rivers, and live there at least a while. By July 12, Winthrop, Dudley, Bradstreet, and the other men were there, staying in the Great House built the year before.[6] It was not spacious, but it had two rooms up and two rooms down.[7] Anne, her mother and sisters, and the other women remained in Salem temporarily until the men could make whatever living arrangements they could.

The captains of later arriving ships informed Governor Winthrop that the French might be planning an attack on the colony. As a protective measure, since they did not yet have a fortification that could contain all the colonists, Winthrop and Dudley decided to place the people throughout the area: some in Boston, others in Charlestown, and still others in nearby Roxbury and Dorchester.[8] (Because many early names of the towns changed, present-day names are used here unless otherwise noted.) The few simple houses that were built were for the more well-to-do men and their families. The wattle-and-daub cottages had thatched roofs and chimneys made of wood and covered with clay.[9] Some people constructed huts of branches and turf; others lived in bark wigwams, which they fashioned like the wigwams of the Native Americans, or tents they made from sailcloth. Most in the latter category included workmen, servants, and former indentured servants. More than one hundred indentured servants had to be released by the Massachusetts Bay Company from their terms of service when the company could not provide enough food or shelter for them; they had to fend for themselves.[10]

No less important than taking care of their physical needs was providing care for their spiritual needs. To that point, they had kept up weekly sermons and daily prayers and Scripture reading. July 30, 1630, was proclaimed a day of fasting and prayer, and a covenant was drawn up to form the church in Charlestown. The people desired to unite themselves "into one congregation or Church, under the Lord Jesus Christ our Head," and they promised to conform to "His holy Ordinances."[11] Historians have pointed out that they did *not* pledge to be conformed to the Church of England. They also chose not to use the Book of Common Prayer; their prayers were to be fresh and new instead of the same ones read and repeated again and again in services.[12] These American Puritans had a Congregational church polity; that is, they controlled local church policy and elected the minister.[13]

Over the next two days, ninety men *and* women signed the covenant. Thomas Dudley and Simon Bradstreet were among the first. It was August 1 before Anne and her mother signed it; they must have still been in Salem on July 30. Despite her many misgivings about being in the new land, Anne later wrote that she "was convinced it was the way of God" and she "submitted to it and joined to the church."[14] Before long, the Charlestown church relocated to Boston and became the First Church of Boston.[15]

The church's organization was completed on August 27, and there was another fast. The Great House was too small to accommodate all the worshippers for the service led by Rev. John Wilson, so they gathered under a large tree at the top of a sloped hill.[16]

In between the two church-related meetings, the Court of Assistants met on August 23 to determine the pay and housing provisions for Rev. Wilson and another minister, George Philips; they also set wage rates for the workmen building the dwellings. Although Simon Bradstreet was the youngest assistant, he served as the secretary and recorded the minutes, as he did for most court assemblies.[17] To be clear, this government of the colony was *not* a theocracy; ministers were not permitted to hold governmental positions, but they were consulted often on matters before the court.

The number of colonists decreased as illnesses ended their earthly pilgrimage. One hopes that they reached the understanding as Anne described it: "When I come into Heaven, I shall understand perfectly what [the Lord] hath done for me, and then shall I be able to praise him as I ought."[18] A poor diet, especially the salty meats, and the lack of warmth had a lot to do with the deaths at sea. Then on land the intense heat of summer was almost more than many could bear; a Massachusetts summer was unlike anything the English men and women had known. Boston had plenty of fresh water, but not all locations shared that good fortune. And then there were the mosquitoes. By the end of the year, more than two hundred new immigrants had perished (either on land or at sea).[19]

To the dismay of the Bradstreets and the Dudleys, their family friend Lady Arbella died in Salem during August. Within a month, her twenty-nine-year-old husband, Isaac Johnson, died too. They had been married seven years but had no children.[20] One historian wrote eloquently about the death of Lady Arbella: "She came from a paradise of plenty and pleasure, which she enjoyed in the family of a noble earldom, into a wilderness of wants," and "she took in New England on her way to heaven."[21] The colony lost two guiding lights: he in governmental and business affairs, and she in social and domestic life.

The colony lost others in the fall when about one hundred

people packed up and left Massachusetts for England or Ireland. Either they were displeased that the new government was shaping up to be too restrictive, or they were worried about starving to death. As the New England winter approached, the notion of starving was more than a possibility. The colonists had to adjust to a diet vastly different from what they had left behind in England, and sometimes there was not much of it. Anne and Simon might have had visions of boiled beef and chicken dancing through their heads—and maybe a nice loaf of bread made from wheat—but sometimes what they got were salt meat and hard tack left from the voyage.[22]

Bounty from the sea and wild game were available, but someone had to catch it or hunt it down. As the weather got colder, doing both became increasingly difficult. They had several varieties of fish, oysters, clams, mussels, and lobsters; one lobster caught that year was said to weigh twenty-five pounds. Eels were roasted, fried, and boiled and flavored with herbs. A more exotic treatment was to stuff the eels with nutmeg and cloves if one was thoughtful enough to have brought those spices from England and they were not spoiled during the voyage.[23] Hunters bagged deer, rabbits, and ducks and other birds.

Thanks to the Native Americans, the colonists learned about corn and how to use it. At various times, the table that Anne shared with her husband and extended family bore hominy and succotash, hoe cakes or ash cakes, and roasted corn. Popcorn was a novelty. To make hasty pudding, they cooked cornmeal in water until it thickened. Wheat was unavailable early on because of blight, so they used rye meal mixed with cornmeal to make bread.[24] Pumpkins were available, but many people did not like them. Perhaps the most common dish was pease porridge, which was field peas boiled or baked to mush and served for all three meals. Favorite foods were mushrooms and berries.[25] As John Winthrop wrote his wife, "Our fare be coarse in respect of what we formerly had," but God made it wholesome.[26]

The colonists had about two hundred cattle as the winter months approached, much fewer than the desired number.[27] They had lost half the cows and most of the goats at sea, and that loss affected their pocketbooks as well as their stomachs because they had to send ships for more. Gradually they imported more cattle, goats, pigs, and chickens from Europe.

Even if they had food in one area, transporting it to another was difficult unless the needy area was near the sea and the goods could be delivered by boat. Because most mares had been lost at sea, horses were scarce. For most people, foot travel was a necessity. An adequate road system that carts could maneuver would take some time and manpower to develop.

The General Court had to deal with more pressing issues than road building from October to December. One was the franchise (the right to vote), and another was an out-of-control would-be colonist, Thomas Morton. At the General Court in October, more than one hundred colonists asked for the vote, and all were allowed. (All, of course, were men.) After that, however, any male who wanted to be a freeman (a voter) had to be a church *member*, not just a churchgoer. It was agreed that the freemen would elect the assistants, and from the assistants they would elect the governor and deputy governor. Then the governor, deputy governor, and assistants would have the power to make laws and choose officers to carry out those laws.[28]

One of the more curious cases of these early days centered on Thomas Morton of Merry Mount, and he surely was a topic around the dinner table for the Bradstreets and Dudleys. A lawyer and aspiring trader, he had come to Plymouth Colony in 1624. He and others in the group that arrived that year soon had disagreements with the Plymouth colonists and founded their own colony, at the site of present-day Quincy. When most of that group left the newly settled area, Morton and a few others remained behind and renamed it Mare Mount (or Merry Mount). Their behavior was so offensive to the Plymouth colonists that they arrested Morton and sent him packing to England in 1627. What was so offensive to them? Among other things, the Merry Mount group set up a maypole to celebrate May Day and danced around it in drunken revelry. Morton had returned to New England by 1630 and wasted no time in getting into more trouble, this time with the court of Massachusetts Bay Colony.

Thomas Dudley summed up what happened: a "multitude of complaints were received against him for injuries done by him both to the English and Indians; and amongst others, for shooting hail-shot at a troop of Indians for not bringing a canoe unto him to cross a river." He hurt one Native American, and his shot went through the "garments" of others. For his misdeeds, the court ordered him to be bound and his goods seized to pay for his transport to England and for restitution to the Native Americans for the canoe. The Massachusetts Bay colonists burned his house to the ground and kept him prisoner until a ship arrived in December to take him away. He wrote *New English Canaan* about his experiences, but he came back again in 1643 and was arrested and jailed in Boston. He died in Maine three years later.[29] For this act and others, the colony became known for its determination not to allow mistreatment of Native Americans.

Their attention to such legal matters is amazing since the colonists were in survival mode. The weather in December was unusually severe, and they were so short of food that some were gathering and eating acorns. Then in early February the *Lion* returned from England bearing grain, beef in barrels, peas, and lemon juice (to prevent scurvy).[30] February 22 was declared a general day of Thanksgiving for the ship's safe arrival. But the *Lion* also brought dire news. There had been many deaths on their ships returning to England the previous year because they had to fight the Dunkirkers. Also, some of the returnees delivered "false and scandalous reports" of the colony, and many in England believed them.[31]

By spring 1631, nearly a year after their arrival, things were looking up for the colonists. A ferry was established between Boston and Charlestown,[32] and Winthrop and the assistants had ordered the deepening of a creek that ran from the Charles River into Newtowne so that boats could convey passengers and freight. They planted crops and started to build dwellings.

In the fall of 1630, Winthrop, the Dudleys, the Bradstreets, and the rest of the assistants had moved to Boston with plans to go to Newtowne in the spring.[33] Newtowne, which is present-day Cambridge, was chosen to be the capital of the colony. It was fortified with a stockade fence for protection, and the gridiron plan for the town was laid out. Governor Winthrop's house was framed there—it was likely two stories tall and had garrets—and he had seven or eight servants living in it. Smaller houses for the Dudleys and Bradstreets were also under construction.

But a disagreement arose between Deputy Governor Dudley and Governor Winthrop. Dudley went to Newtowne "with the express agreement that the government and the capital were to be removed there."[34] Then Winthrop decided that the seat of government should be in Boston, and he had his house taken down and moved to Boston.[35] Most of the other assistants chose to live in Boston too.

It was not the last time the two leaders butted heads; Dudley was said to have "hardness in public and rigidity in private life" and to be irascible.[36] His daughter Anne did not agree with that view, of course—although she allowed that not all would equally esteem him. She wrote, "Well known and loved, where ere he lived, by most / Both in his native, and in foreign coast."[37]

At last in July 1631, the Dudleys, Bradstreets, and six other families moved into the first eight houses in Newtowne.[38] Anne and Simon had been without a real home since they left England seventeen months earlier.

A HOME AT LAST

nne's expectation of being able to move with Simon into a home of their own, however humble, had been dashed just after the *Arbella* anchored. The two Bradstreets had crowded into a dwelling in Boston with the six members of the Dudley family, and they were glad to have that until houses could be built for them. They had few comforts and little furniture, but more than enough togetherness.

Thomas Dudley gently complained about having to write letters on his knee, using the fireside for light, because he had "yet no table nor other room to write in." He was surrounded by family members in the main room, where they ate meals and spent their days, and he added, "They break good manners, and make me many times forget what I would say, and say what I would not."[1] Now, in July 1631, the families had separate homes in Newtowne.

The Dudleys' house on one-half acre was at the present-day corner of Dunster and South Streets, which was just a few blocks away from the Bradstreets. Dunster Street was the principal street of the town. Anne and Simon set up housekeeping on a one-quarter-acre lot at the present-day address of 1380 Massachusetts Avenue in Cambridge. The house was in what is now Harvard Square, and the cow pasture next door was in what is now Harvard Yard.[2]

The term *Mistress* was reserved for prominent or wealthy women; others in lower station were called *Goodwife* or *Goody*. Mistress Bradstreet's home in Newtowne was not as large as her mother's as wife of the deputy governor, but it was hers to run. Both women had servants, as did Governor Winthrop, but not as many as he had. Their frame houses were covered with weatherboarding, and oiled paper covered the window spaces until leaded glass could be shipped from England and installed. About two years later, Governor Winthrop upbraided Deputy Governor Dudley because he thought Dudley had overly adorned his house with wainscoting. He was not setting a good example for others, said Winthrop, when there were so many things to do in the colony; besides that, it must have been costly. Dudley responded that it was only clapboard, done in the style of wainscoting, added for the "warmth" of the house.[3] A family dog or two were stretched out in front of the houses because several dogs had traveled on the *Arbella*.[4]

The furniture and other household items were sparse until more came from England. At the least, Anne and Simon had a table for meals, a cupboard for tableware and other items, stools or benches, and a bed. The stone fireplace warmed the house and was used for cooking. Early on, Anne filled the lamps with fish oil, and her candlesticks held candles that the servants made of bayberry wax. Lacking fish oil or candles, some colonists burned thinly sliced pieces of wood from pine trees, which were full of turpentine and pitch.[5]

The conditions awaiting the Puritan immigrants to Massachusetts were far from ideal, but the worsening conditions for them in England pushed them into the ships bound for the New World. Writing to Lady Bridget about life in the colony, Thomas Dudley said, "If any come hither for worldly ends, that can live well at home [in England], he commits an error . . . but if for spiritual, and that no particular obstacle hinder his removal, he may well find here what may well content him." He listed wood to burn, plenty of materials for building homes, ground to plant, seas and rivers with fish, pure air, and "fowl and venison, they are dainties here as well as in England." They were enduring a lot, he admitted, but he could see ahead to better times in the land.[6]

The Puritans believed that hard work was a virtue, but it was not to be divided into the secular and the sacred. All jobs done well could glorify God. If God blessed someone's work with prosperity, then God's grace, "not human merit," produced the blessing.[7] Englishman William Wood spent time in the developing colony and wrote, "Many do disparage the land, saying a man cannot live without labor; in that they more disparage and discredit themselves, in giving the world occasion to take notice of their dronish disposition, that would live off the sweat of another man's brows." Too many had arrived without the means or willingness to provide for themselves and thought that they could "live in plenty and idleness." There was so much work to be done that Wood encouraged readers "of weak constitutions" to stay in England if they could not afford servants. They needed money to transport animals and household goods and to pay for building houses and planting and gathering crops. "For all New-England must be workers in some kind."[8]

The work for Thomas Dudley and Simon Bradstreet was related to the Massachusetts Bay Colony, and they had to make the two-mile trek to Boston whenever court met or other colony business required them. They likely took a boat as often as they could instead of walking.[9] Despite Governor Winthrop's notions, Dudley remained convinced that Boston was not the proper place for the seat of government. Fences could not be erected to protect cows because of the marshes in one area. There were so few woods and meadows that they had to ship in timber and hay on boats. On the other hand, there were no rattlesnakes, and gardens and cornfields thrived with plenty of fresh water available. Since it was the governor's place of residence, it remained the seat of government—for a while.[10]

The arrival in November 1631 of Winthrop's wife, Margaret, and some of his children might have had something to do with his firm decision not to leave Boston. The list of items that he requested them to bring included necessities for colonial life: linens and woolens, bedding, brass and pewter wares, leather bottles, axes and tools, soap, candles, foodstuffs (oatmeal, peas, cheese), leather shoes and stockings for the children, hats, and other clothing. Sheep, goats, and milk cows were also on his list.[11] He had long awaited his family, and his delight at seeing them had to be tempered by his distress at learning that on the voyage, his daughter Ann, who was born after he came to Massachusetts, died and was buried at sea.

Margaret was not Winthrop's first wife. His first wife, Mary, had been the source of a major portion of his sizable estate, and she was the mother of six of his children. He provided the best possible for all of his children and Margaret, even in the early days of the colony. He made sure that she had both male and female servants to help her. Some were Native Americans, but there is no indication that he used "Moores" (blacks) as servants in his household. Yet like all wives, Mistress Winthrop had plenty of duties, and she baked her own bread and fetched water from the nearby spring.[12]

Anne's only brother, Samuel, lost no time in getting to know Mary Winthrop, daughter of the governor. At age twenty-four, he married her in 1632. In keeping with Puritan ways, they did not exchange rings, and a magistrate, not a pastor, married them.[13] The young couple built a house in Newtowne, near his family members. Later they moved to Ipswich, and then Samuel was a founder of Salisbury, where he was in the General Court for several years. Mary died in childbirth, after which Samuel had two more wives. Samuel and his family last settled in New Hampshire, where he was a preacher, although he was noted to be among the first to "attempt to improve the breed of horses, cattle, and sheep" in New England.[14] The marriage of Mary and Samuel brought together their fathers into the in-law relationship, and although their differences did not disappear, they were toned down. Both men remained among the eminent leadership of the colony as long as they lived.

The family circle grew when Anne's sister Patience, age sixteen, married Daniel Denison in October 1632, and they too built a house in Newtowne. Daniel was another Cambridge graduate, and he eventually became the major general of Massachusetts Bay and served in the General Court.

The first meetinghouse in Newtowne, near the Dudleys' home, was not built until 1633. Its pastor was Rev. Thomas Hooker, newly arrived from Holland after fleeing England. Until that time, the people of Newtowne went to Boston for services. The congregation that was first established in Charlestown and led by John Wilson had moved to Boston when the governor and the assistants moved in September 1630. It had no meetinghouse until 1632: it was a simple unheated structure of mud walls, a thatched roof, and an earthen floor, and the congregation sat on wooden benches.[15]

Anne was unable to go to Boston for services for some time, however, because she was once more beset by a disabling illness. Within just a few months of their move to Newtowne, after the first of the year, 1632, Anne's fragile constitution must have had all it could take with the new surroundings, food, and climate. Even with her mother's help and advice, she was trying to set up a household with more than the usual challenges. She also had to run the whole household in Simon's too-frequent absences, and she never got used to him being away from her. In spiritual terms, men and women were equal in Puritanism, but the hierarchy in the home was functional: somebody had to make final decisions, and that was the husband if he was home. The wife had to make adjustments when she was the one left in charge.

After her recovery, Anne wrote about the incident. She was stricken by a "lingering sickness like a consumption" complicated by "lameness." At twenty years of age, she was convinced that her mortal race was run and she was approaching "fatal Death." Just as she had felt in her earlier illnesses, she felt that God was trying to humble her, and "it was not altogether ineffectual." It was not pleasant: she felt "wasting pains" as she tossed on her "wakeful bed, / Bedrenched with tears that flowed from mournful head." Finally she had no more tears. She looked up to the throne of the one who sends "help to those in misery," and he eased her soul of woe and her flesh of pain.[16]

Yet a new woe must have hovered in the back of Anne's mind when she heard her father and husband talk about relocating. By August 1632, Newtowne was becoming crowded, and there were not enough places for newcomers to build. Anne had barely gotten established in Newtowne and was trying to get back on her feet after her illness, and they were already sending out men to survey new places in the colony to settle. They decided that Ipswich (then called Agawam) was a likely prospect about thirty miles north of Newtowne as the crow flies; it was really "out there" in terms of being far from other settled areas. The men dropped the discussion about moving—for a while. That was not the last Anne heard of leaving Newtowne, but soon she had something dear to her heart to occupy her time and thoughts: motherhood.

6

"IT PLEASED GOD"

"It pleased God to keep me a long time without a child, which was a great grief to me, and cost me many prayers and tears before I obtained one, and after him gave me many more of whom I now take the care,"[1] wrote Anne. Her first child, Samuel, was born in 1633, the year after she feared her life was at an end and five years after she married Simon.

The anticipation of the birth of her child brought with it a lot of apprehension and a lot of preparation. For someone with Anne's medical history, even carrying a child to term was a gift of God and an answer to prayer. Anne's mother and other women in the community planned to be ready even before the child's birth for Anne's lying-in. The most important member of the party was the midwife. The rest of the women cared for Anne and the household for three to four weeks until she was allowed out of bed and could resume her usual duties. If she could, she would nurse Samuel for up to a year. Anne and Simon had to provide food for what could be a crowd; one prominent New England woman had seventeen helpers at her lying-in. A "groaning party" was held for the women because the table groaned under the weight of all the food on it and because the name honored what the new mother had just been through. And a cradle, gowns and caps, and blankets for the baby had to be made.

The fear of a newborn's death was realistic, but demographic studies done since the late 1970s have found that a child born in an inland town of Massachusetts during the colonial period had a higher survival rate than a child born on the seacoast and higher still than a child born in England. Some of that had to do with infectious diseases being found more often at the coasts and in urban English areas not known for sanitary conditions.[2]

We have a clue about Anne's philosophy of child rearing from her statement, "Diverse children have their different natures . . . those parents are wise that can fit their nurture according to their Nature."[3] She recognized that her children had different personalities, as well as different strengths and weaknesses, and she eventually applied this understanding to her and Simon's four boys and four girls. Of course, she incorporated this flexibility with a firmness about the basic behaviors expected of her children as young Puritans.

The happiness that Samuel's birth brought to his parents, grandparents, aunts, and uncles was dampened by fresh news in 1633 about the tribulations of the Puritans in England. Bishop Laud had become archbishop of Canterbury and had gained even more power. With his elevation of status, the English immigrants flowed instead of trickled into Massachusetts.

An unforgettable example of what could happen was that of Puritan writer and lawyer William Prynne. Laud had Prynne arrested, tried, and imprisoned for writing a pamphlet that Laud regarded as seditious. The sentence also ordered that both of Prynne's ears were to be cut off. Prynne was not to be stopped, however, and continued to write, smuggling his pamphlets out of the Tower of London. As further punishment, the stumps of his ears were shorn off and the letters *SL* (seditious libeler) were branded on his cheeks.[4] After that, Prynne was imprisoned *again* in a different prison, and he was not freed until 1640.

John Cotton was a most welcome old friend of the Dudleys and Bradstreets from St. Botolph's Church in Lincolnshire. He was another target of Laud but managed to escape to London before sailing to Boston, Massachusetts, and arriving there in September 1633. He brought his wife and children with him, and a son, named Seaborn, was born on the voyage.

Within a few weeks, Cotton was named teacher at the First Church of Boston, where John Wilson was the pastor. A church of any size in Massachusetts strived to have men in both positions. The men visited members of the flock and sometimes intervened in disputes among neighbors.[5] In the services, the pastor offered warning or advice or encouraged listeners, and the teacher explained the doctrine. There were two sermons on Sunday and lectures during the week, and church members were expected to be present for all meetings. Puritan sermons were always in English, not Latin.

There was to be no work on Sunday (actually from sunset Saturday to sunset Sunday), so a Sunday in Boston followed a predictable pattern. A bell summoned people to the worship service in the meetinghouse that began around 9:00 a.m. (In other towns, a drum was beaten to summon them.) The men and women entered separately and sat on opposite sides. The pastor delivered a prayer, and the teacher read a chapter in the Bible. The congregation sang a psalm, with *all* verses, whether it was a long one, such as Psalm 119, or a short one, such as Psalm 120. There were no instruments and no professional singers; it was congregational singing. The congregation usually stood during the psalms and prayers. Next came the sermon with the pastor's brief explanation and application to everyday life. The teacher offered a prayer and a blessing, and the meeting was dismissed until around 2:00 p.m. so that everyone could eat. The break was also a social one, a time for visiting with friends who had come from the surrounding areas.

When the people reconvened, the pastor offered another prayer, another psalm was sung, and the teacher delivered a sermon. The teacher might also read and expound on another chapter of the Bible before the sermon. More prayers might be interspersed throughout the meeting.[6]

One of John Cotton's Sunday sermons covered the following scriptures from the Old and New Testaments: all chapters of the books of Ecclesiastes and Zephaniah, and chapters 1–6 in the gospel of John. During the Lord's Supper, which was usually held every month, he preached on 1 Corinthians 11, 2 Chronicles 30, and other verses.[7] His and other Puritan ministers' lengthy sermons presented doctrinal points with quotations from the Bible, and the ministers might cite explanations of the original languages of Scripture.[8] A professor observed that these sermons demanded a lot of the preacher and the congregation, and "Puritan clergy came as close to being an intellectual ruling class—or, more properly, a class of intellectuals intimately associated with a ruling power—as America ever had."[9] Very often congregants took notes so that they could discuss the sermons at home.[10]

Children accompanied their parents to services, and Anne took infant Samuel as soon as she could leave the house. That the older children were expected to sit still and behave during the daylong outing boggles the mind, no matter how much they wanted to obey their parents and the Lord. The girls usually sat with the women, but the boys were in a separate section on a low bench under the watchful eyes of the tithing man— just in case their rowdiness overcame their better natures.

If a child was to be baptized, the baptism came at the end of the day, just before the offering. The pastor gave a speech or discussed baptism and the duties of the church and the parents or both in bringing up the child in the faith. The child would be washed or sprinkled. A child could not be baptized unless both parents were members of the church.

Offerings were given according to one's rank in town: magistrates and gentlemen first, then the rest of the married men, then single men and women, widows, and wives whose husbands were out of town.[11]

While maintaining the importance of lectures by the pastor or teacher, the General Court was compelled to issue restrictions on them early in October 1633 because of the time taken away from regular duties: "It is found by common experience that the keeping of lectures at the ordinary hours now observed in the forenoon to be divers ways prejudicial to the common good, both in the loss of a whole day and bringing other charges and troubles to the place where the lecture is kept," so it was ordered that no lecture was to begin before 1:00 p.m. Later on, the court ordered lectures to be held only on Thursdays.[12]

Teaching the catechism to children was essential, and John Cotton prepared one for them. "Milk for Babes" had the subtitle "Drawn Out of the Breasts of Both Testaments. Chiefly, for the Spirituall Nourishment of Boston Babes in Either England: But May Be of Like Use for Any Children," and it presented sixty-four questions and answers. It dealt with the chief end of man; the purpose of the Scriptures; explanations of justification, sanctification, and grace; the meaning of the Godhead of three; the decrees of God; original sin; the Ten Commandments; proper behavior on the Sabbath; and the meaning of baptism and the Lord's Supper. All were heady concepts for children, and not all were as simply stated as these two questions and answers:

> Q: What are the wages of sin?
> A: Death and damnation.
> Q: How can you be saved?
> A: Only by Jesus Christ.

Then consider this:

> Q: What is effectual calling?
> A: Effectual calling is the work of God's Spirit, whereby convincing us of our sin and misery, enlightening our minds in the knowledge of Christ, and renewing our wills, he doth persuade and enable us to embrace Jesus Christ, freely offered to us in the gospel.[13]

Spiritual nourishment was not just for "babes" in Boston. It was also the point of Puritan sermons instructing listeners that they must not lose the constant battle between the flesh and the spirit. In her poem "The Flesh and the Spirit," Anne wrestled with the same subject that the apostle Paul wrote about in Galatians 5:17: "The flesh lusteth against the Spirit, and the Spirit against the flesh: and these are contrary the one to the other: so that ye cannot do the things that ye would." She set up the poem as two sisters, Flesh and Spirit, discussing "things that are past, and things to come" in a "deadly feud."[14] Spirit was the clear winner.

Flesh was obsessed with wealth and vanity while Spirit lived on meditation. Adam was Flesh's father, but Spirit's Father was from above.

Flesh taunted Spirit by saying:

Doth Contemplation feed thee so
Regardlessly to let earth go?
Can Speculation satisfy
Notion without Reality?
Dost dream of things beyond the Moon
And dost thou hope to dwell there soon? . . .
For riches doth thou long full sore?
Behold enough of precious store.
Earth hath more silver, pearls and gold,
Than eyes can see, or hands can hold.
Affects thou pleasure? take thy fill,
Earth hath enough of what you will.
Then let not go, what thou mayest find,
For things unknown, only in mind.

Spirit responded,

Be still thou unregenerate part,
Disturb no more my settled heart,
For I have vowed (and so will do)
Thee as a foe, still to pursue.
And combat with thee will and must,
Until I see thee laid in the dust.
Sisters we are, yea twins we be,
Yet deadly feud 'twixt thee and me. . . .
Thy sinful pleasures I do hate,
Thy riches are to me no bait. . . .
For my ambition lies above.
My greatest honor it shall be
When I am victor over thee. . . .
The City where I hope to dwell,
There's none on Earth can parallel; . . .
This City pure is not for thee,
For things unclean there shall not be:
If I of Heaven may have my fill,
Take thou the world, and all that will.[15]

Despite social critic H. L. Mencken's derogatory comment that "Puritanism is the haunting fear that someone, somewhere, may be happy,"[16] the Puritans were not a dour bunch or opposed to having fun. Although musical instruments were not permitted in churches, owning an instrument and playing it at home or using it in a military ceremony was acceptable. They approved of sports or recreation, such as hunting, fishing, reading, skating, and archery, but games of chance, card playing, and horse racing were off-limits.[17] They did rest; they were not workaholics. But as we have learned, there was a lot of work to be done in establishing a colony and not much time for amusements.

Dancing was not encouraged, but Rev. John Cotton ruled that it was not all wrong because there was no specific biblical prohibition. He was equally clear in denouncing "lascivious dancing, and amorous gestures and wanton dalliances."[18]

Puritans did not exist in a world of black and white when it came to clothing or houses, although most ministers did wear black and men sometimes wore broad-brimmed black felt hats.[19] John Endicott used scarlet paint on the trim of his house in Salem. Everyday clothing was gray, green, or dark blue, and people dressed up for special occasions—within limits. Essex County (Ipswich) probate records noted a purple suit, a green doublet, red waistcoats, and blue and red petticoats among the belongings of the deceased.

The General Court apparently thought some colonists were going overboard on finery, though, and ruled:

[N]o person either man or woman shall hereafter make or buy any apparel, either woolen or silk or linen with any lace on it, silver, gold, or thread, under the penalty of forfeiture of said clothes. Also that no person either man or woman shall make or buy any slashed clothes other than one slash in each sleeve and another in the back; also all cut-works, embroideries, or needlework caps, bands, and rails are forbidden hereafter to be made and worn under the aforesaid penalty: also all gold or silver girdles, hatbands, belts, ruffs, beaverhats are prohibited to be bought and worn hereafter.[20]

Other forbidden clothing included double ruffles and capes. In 1651, a ban was placed on "great boots" for men and women. These restrictions had no effect on Anne, who was not known for ostentatious dressing; if anything, she dressed more conservatively than most women of her age and social status.

Long hairstyles for men were considered "a wile of the devil," and Puritans cited the apostle Paul's comment: "Doth not even nature itself teach you, that, if a man have long hair, it is a shame unto him? But if a woman have long hair, it is a glory to her: for her hair is given her for a covering" (1 Cor. 11:14–15). These rules about clothing and hairstyles were not as strictly enforced as ones involving stealing or inflicting bodily harm on others. Most clothing and hairstyle rules were directed at discouraging undue attention to anything that inspired one's vanity.[21]

As for holidays, Anne and her family did not celebrate Christmas or Easter. Puritans forbade the celebration of both because Scripture did not sanction either holiday, and Christmas especially was known in England and France for encouraging excesses of eating and drinking and other riotous merrymaking. Besides that, they regarded all days as holy, not one or two special days on the calendar.

Thanksgiving was not reserved for a single day in the year; there were as many days of thanksgiving as there were special positive events. The colonists celebrated a general thanksgiving in mid-February 1631 because the much anticipated ship arrived with food and other provisions. In early October 1633, there was a general thanksgiving because they brought in a good harvest and several ships arrived safely, bringing more goods and people. They also turned building a house or a meetinghouse into a celebration. A fast was held when catastrophe struck or seemed imminent, such as when they were experiencing a severe drought. Or a day of fasting and prayer was held when something spiritual was happening, as on the day in July 1630 when the covenant was drawn up to form the church in Charlestown.

One approved major civic holiday was muster or training day (for training the militia). The General Court ordered the formation of a militia in 1630. Able-bodied men were to serve, and all adult males except ministers and magistrates were to possess arms.[22] The days were not regularly scheduled, but there were usually about a half dozen a year, in the spring and fall; the frequency often depended on threats to the colony. The families accompanied the men to the site, and the women and children and older men watched the drills. Then food was served in the middle of the day, and in the afternoon, the young men might face off in wrestling matches or foot races.

Another approved and very important civic holiday was election day. Following a procession of government officials to the meetinghouse, a minister delivered an election day sermon discussing the nature of government as set out in the Bible, the duties of rulers, and the general need for personal reformation, but the sermon did not endorse specific candidates. Simon Bradstreet, though still a young man, was increasingly recognized for his competence in governmental affairs. At a meeting of the townspeople, he was elected as one of six selectmen to transact Newtowne business.

Election day in the summer of 1634 proved a victory for Anne's father, who had been deputy governor since 1630. He was elected governor of Massachusetts Bay Colony, defeating John Winthrop. While he served his one-year term as governor, the General Court and colony business operations moved to Newtowne and remained there for one more year with the election of a new governor in 1635. Then the operations went back again to Boston.[23] Although he served three more times as governor (1640, 1645, 1650, all one-year terms), Dudley was a proponent of rotation in office. The last thing that New England needed, he thought, was one man with all the power, as a king had.

To that point, King Charles's government and Archbishop Laud had left Massachusetts alone for the most part, but that did not mean they intended to stay on that path. With ships going back and forth from the colony to England, each side could keep track of the other through letters and messengers. Some "disaffected" people in England informed Archbishop Laud and the Privy Council that the Puritans, "among other wrong-doings, were setting up in America an independent church and state," wrote Augustine Jones, Thomas Dudley's biographer. The first action by the royal government was to stop ships bound for Massachusetts and force the passengers to take an oath of allegiance to the Crown and to be conformed to the Prayer Book. The next was to set up a commission, led by Archbishop Laud, to hear complaints against the colonists and basically to prepare to take over the American colonies.[24]

Learning about that, Governor Dudley and other leaders of Massachusetts started preparing for war against England. No one questioned the wisdom of a new colony, populated by comparatively few citizens, making such plans. No one had to state aloud that they would be facing a formidable force. The court granted Governor Dudley, John Winthrop, John Endicott, and two others "power to consult, direct, and give command for the managing and ordering of any war that may befall us, for a space of a year next ensuing and till further order be taken herein."[25] They armed and trained the militia and fortified the towns. They kept a lookout on duty around the clock on Beacon Hill in Boston to warn of incoming warships.

Anne trusted her father to do what was right for the well-being of the colony, and she knew that he had experience in warfare from his youth. As always, he would not be put off by a challenge, no matter how great. But as she observed or heard about the preparations for armed conflict, she must have prayed that there would be no alarm calling everyone to arms to fight British troops assaulting the towns of Massachusetts.

Then it happened. It was not a warning shot from Beacon Hill but a letter from the Crown to the General Court. In September, the Massachusetts Bay Colony was ordered to lay its charter before the Privy Council in London, in effect turning over the government to the Crown. Charles I and the archbishop underestimated the colonists' legal expertise and understanding of delaying tactics, however. The colonists responded that only the General Court could act on the request, and the next meeting of the court was not scheduled until September of the *next* year. Each time a demand came from the Crown, the colonists sent another letter, offering another valid excuse to avoid handing over the charter, and time worked in their favor.

The political situation within England soon took the Crown's attention off the colony and onto domestic affairs that were proving more than the government could handle. Charles I's subjects were angry with him because he tried to levy a tax, called ship money, on the whole country and because there was still no Parliament (which Charles I had dissolved in 1620). Laud was intensifying pressure on Puritans within the country, and some were leaving for the New World while others were digging in to resist. Laud also had his eye on the churches in Scotland, and he attempted to make them forsake their Presbyterianism and conform to the Church of England. But the Scottish people had had enough, and they opposed Laud and Charles, eventually confronting the king's troops.

While the political kettle in England was starting to simmer and come to a boil that was the civil war, the summer of 1634 brought another much-loved family to Boston from England: Lady Arbella's sister, Lady Susan Humphrey; her husband, John; and their three daughters and one son. Much to Anne's disappointment, they did not remain in Boston. Within the year, they moved to Lynn, about nine miles north of Boston on Massachusetts Bay, and John became a magistrate there.

Lady Susan must have had reservations about coming to a place where her sister and brother-in-law and many others she knew had died so young. But her husband had a vested interest in the colony, and she likely did not have much choice. She stayed seven years and apparently was homesick from the first day in New England, maybe from the moment she started packing to leave England. Anne and her mother and her siblings probably saw Lady Susan very little because of the distance separating them. She never adjusted to colonial life with its absence of the elegant surroundings to which she had become accustomed; she became "weary of the privations of the wilderness"; and she feared the Native Americans. Her husband's fortunes were waning, too, with financial losses in investments in the Bahamas.

To satisfy her, John Humphrey sold most of his farm holdings in Lynn and took Lady Susan back to England at the end of October 1641. They left the children in Massachusetts because they planned to go by way of the Bahamas, and given the time of year, the parents feared that severe weather might befall them. They thought the children were safer in Massachusetts, and they placed them in the care of a couple, Jenkin Davis and his wife. Davis was a trusted member of the Lynn church and had been an employee of the Humphreys. The community severely criticized the parents for leaving the children, no matter what the reason. In the nineteenth century, historians were still berating the parents for their neglect of the children.

The wickedness that occurred in the parents' absence was almost unheard-of in a colony that stressed keeping the flesh under control. Most historical narratives written at the time do not describe what happened other than to say that two of the daughters, Dorcas and Sarah, were involved in a tragedy or misfortune. In truth both girls, under the age of nine, were sexually abused for up to a year by three men, one of whom was Davis. Usually the abuse occurred on Sunday or lecture day. There was a trial, and the General Court—including Anne Bradstreet's father and her husband—was divided about the sentence for the men. Some members wanted to execute the perpetrators, but there was no law in the colony dealing with such a crime to permit them to do that. All three men were fined, whipped with forty stripes, and imprisoned for a time. One also had his nostrils slit, and another had to wear a rope around his neck until the General Court told him to remove it; if he ever repeated his crime, he was to be executed.

Lady Susan and her husband never returned to Massachusetts. Records are unclear about who cared for the children after the trial. There is some evidence that Dorcas was placed with a family in Boston and as an adult went to France, then England, and died back in Massachusetts. Sarah likely died as a teen. Daughter Ann, who was not abused, married and inherited some of the family lands in Lynn. The Humphreys had had two more boys while in New England, so there were three sons when the parents left. By 1681, Ann was the only surviving child.[26]

Anne Bradstreet likely shared Lady Susan's unease with the wilderness, and when she heard her father and her husband again discuss a move to Ipswich, the most remote settlement in the Massachusetts Bay Colony, her heart must have risen in protest once more. By 1635, there were eighty-six houses in Newtowne, and conditions were more crowded because of the influx of immigrants.[27] Her father had served his term as governor, he was needed in Ipswich, and he was ready to take his extended family with him into the wilderness.[28]

Anne prepared to move to yet another place where she had no desire to go. But in that wilderness, her Muse took flight, and Anne wrote most of her poems in Ipswich.

IN THE WILDERNESS

Ipswich, founded in 1633, was named for a town in England from which many colonists came. Its Native American name was Agawam. It was about thirty miles northeast of Boston on the banks of a river and near the ocean. To the north and west of Ipswich was a "wild wilderness" of "Indian trails" and wooded areas populated by wolves and bears.[1] John Winthrop Jr. was one of the founders, and when his father, the governor, visited him, he had to walk a hard-to-follow "Indian trail" to get there.[2] Ipswich had fresh water and good fishing, and the beach was a ready source of clams.

It seemed an unlikely place for a poet to call home. Yet one claim to Ipswich's fame was Anne Bradstreet, although she did not seek it and was no longer a resident when the fame came to her. One historian proclaimed that she "dared to claim new honor for her sex"[3] in Ipswich because she wrote most of her poetry while living there from 1635 to 1644. That Anne could write so much while living in a "wild wilderness" and caring for a home and husband and several children is a testament to her need to write and her determination to do it. She and many of her neighbors proved that, even in a wilderness, the life of the mind could be cultivated. One of those intellectual neighbors was the minister Nathaniel Ward. An acquaintance of Sir Francis Bacon, Ward was another graduate of Emmanuel College, Cambridge.[4]

The street names described the physical conditions in the new settlement: Dirty Lane was almost like a swamp, and Hog Lane was where the hogs roamed. Even after more settlers came, the roads were not much more than wheel ruts with grass in between.[5] Until fences were erected, cows had to be watched carefully to protect them from wolves.

The burying ground in Ipswich, like that in all Puritan settlements, was not part of a churchyard, and unfortunately the first two people buried were the young wife of John Winthrop Jr. and their infant daughter. He immediately went to England after their deaths, and in 1635, he moved to Connecticut, one of the four major Puritan areas (Plymouth, Massachusetts Bay, Connecticut, and New Haven). The younger Winthrop returned to spend a few more years in Massachusetts Bay Colony, but he eventually made his permanent home in Connecticut, where he held significant governmental positions (the last as governor, 1659–76).[6]

The departure of John Winthrop Jr. left a leadership void, and that was why Thomas Dudley, almost age sixty, was needed since the settlement was so new. Until more houses could be built, the extended family lived in the good-sized home left behind by John Winthrop Jr. Living in the house were Thomas and Dorothy Dudley and their unmarried daughters Sarah and Mercy; Patience and Daniel Denison; Samuel and Mary Dudley; and Anne, Simon, and two-year-old Samuel Bradstreet. Anne and Simon's second child, Dorothy, was born either just before or just after the move to Ipswich.[7]

In 1635, the General Court ordered that in Ipswich no house was to be more than a half mile from the meetinghouse because of the Native American threat. The Native Americans suffered a horrendous smallpox epidemic in 1633–34 throughout New England, and several thousand died despite the colonists' efforts to help them.[8] Although their numbers were reduced, the actions of some Native Americans kept fresh in the colonists' minds what could happen to them.

The meetinghouse was located on a hilltop, and behind it was the stone fort. The whipping post, stocks, and the prison were not far away.[9] The fear of attack was so great that the men took their weapons with them when they went to worship, and ammunition was kept in the meetinghouse. Townspeople could not miss the signal for public alarm if they were out and about during the day: three muskets were fired. At night if they heard a drum beating continuously or a cannon discharged, they knew they could be in for it. And if someone called out, "Arm! Arm!" Anne was to grab her toddler and her infant and run to the fort for safety.[10] Anne's brother-in-law Daniel Denison, who had been a soldier, was appointed the military leader of the community. In 1634, Denison had the grim duty of informing Ipswich about a tragedy in another colony. A group of Europeans were killed in Connecticut by a tribe associated with the Pequots (pronounced *pea-kwats*). To try to smooth things over, the Pequots negotiated a treaty with Massachusetts, but the Pequot governing council did not ratify it. Needless to say, the situation troubled the colonists in all of New England. In 1636, several colonists were attacked and killed near Block Island, also in Connecticut, by another tribe associated with the Pequots. In retaliation, John Endicott led an expedition in August that burned Pequot homes and crops, but the people had fled before their arrival. Other tribes joined the colonists in opposition to the Pequots.

The threat intensified throughout the remainder of 1636 and into the next year, and the colonists were ordered to be armed when they traveled. The women and children could not even go to the shore to gather clams unless armed men accompanied them. In the spring of 1637 Plymouth, Massachusetts, and Connecticut agreed to join forces, and in May they attacked a Native American fort and killed from four hundred to seven hundred Pequots within an hour. In 1638, the Treaty of Hartford (which ended the Pequot War) stated, among other restrictions on the survivors, that the Pequot name could no longer be used. The tribe was no more.[11]

Commenting on these events, Alden T. Vaughan wrote, "In 1637 New England's armies gave their Pequot opponents a painful lesson in European military practices. The resulting carnage does not, however, justify charges" by historians that the Puritans meant genocide. The Puritans were fighting what they considered "the Lord's battle."[12]

To their credit, New England governments restricted colonists in land acquisitions from Native Americans. Colonists were supposed to purchase the land, and often the tribes retained hunting and/or fishing rights—and they had the deeds to show it. Laws were passed that did not permit Native Americans to have alcohol or firearms, and prosecutions became common in regard to the trading of guns, ammunition, and liquor. Usually the sellers (the colonists) were the guilty parties. There were some incidents of pigs and cows being stolen, and the Native Americans sold the meat to people in a different colony. When colonists murdered Native Americans, the guilty parties were executed.[13]

After an extensive study, Vaughan discovered that the smaller number of Native Americans in New England compared to the number in other colonies was caused by disease, war among themselves, and migration. Eventually, Native Americans in New England were allowed to be jury members in some cases, and colonists and Native Americans prospered from trade with one another.[14]

In spite of all this turmoil, the Bradstreets, Dudleys, and Denisons built their homes and started new chapters in their lives in the frontier environment. For Anne and her father, at least a small consolation when they first arrived and had to live in the crowded house was access to John Winthrop Jr.'s library of one thousand volumes, including science, math, medicine, and chemistry books; many were in languages other than English.[15] Perhaps the younger Winthrop's love of books came from his father. When Winthrop Sr. built his second house in Boston, his study was filled with Calvin's *Institutes*, a French Bible, prayer books, homilies, books in Latin, sermons, and commentaries on the Bible.[16]

Thomas and Dorothy Dudley had nine acres, and based on assessments, Thomas was the wealthiest man in the colony.[17] Nathaniel Rogers wrote a poem in Latin about Thomas and called him "a devourer of books, in himself a choice collector; a commend of sacred history; a companion for the table, hence eloquent," and "a master of rhetoric."[18] His new house had space for his library, which included fifty or sixty books: histories about Queen Elizabeth I and about wars in France and Scotland, Bibles, works by Calvin and by local ministers, and books on education and theology. Anne obviously used some of his books when writing her longer, historical poems.

The Dudley and Bradstreet homes were considered the center of the community's action. Simon was well liked and was a significant figure in the colony and town government. The Dudleys and Bradstreets must have entertained the neighbors as often as they could, especially Nathaniel Ward; John Norton, the teacher at Ipswich church who had attended Cambridge University and was known for his scholarship; and Nathaniel Rogers, who succeeded Nathaniel Ward as pastor. More than likely, visitors on governmental business ended up in one of their homes. The conversation around their dinner tables must have covered everything from the health of their stock and their business affairs to theological topics, especially those presented in the latest sermon or lecture, to current issues before the General Court.

Some historians paint Puritans as coldhearted beings with no interest in sex, other than to create the next generation. Puritan ministers, however, not only sanctioned sex within marriage but also encouraged it as part of a healthy marital relationship. Sex between unmarried people was another thing altogether, as was adultery. One case was heard before the court when Henry G. solicited another man's wife to adultery while her husband was away. Although she repeatedly turned him down, he went so far as to join her in bed in her home "to her great affright." He was found guilty and faced a sentence of imprisonment, whipping, or a thirty-pound fine.[19]

Church members were apparently not reluctant to talk about sex in public. One wife was so distraught that her husband "denied conjugal fellowship" with her "for the space of two years together" that she took her complaint to her pastor, who then took it to the congregation. The husband was excommunicated because sex within marriage was noted as a "due benevolence."[20]

Simon was a devoted and loving husband and father, and Anne was passionately in love with him. An early biographer of Anne, Helen Campbell, described the love between Anne and Simon as "quiet but fervent."[21] Anne's poetry to him was not intended to be published; it was for his eyes only. We are lucky that it has survived and that her heirs permitted it to be published. The fervor is evident.

Although Anne did not write the following poems to her husband at the same time, reading them together increases their impact. Not all lines are included here, however, because of the poems' length. What must Simon have thought when he read them?

"To My Dear and Loving Husband"

If ever two were one, then surely we.
If ever man were loved by wife, then thee;
If ever wife was happy in a man. . . .
I prize thy love more than whole Mines of gold. . . .
My love is such that Rivers cannot quench,
Nor ought but love from thee, give recompense.
Thy love is such I can no way repay.[22]

Her health issues must have been weighing on her mind when she wrote "Before the Birth of One of Her Children." She and Simon had three more children while living in Ipswich: Sarah (1638), Simon (1640), and Hannah (1642). Anne was thirty when she had Hannah—and she was not their last child. Anne's death was a theme of this poem:

> How soon, my Dear, death may my steps attend,
> How soon't may be thy Lot to lose thy friend.
> We both are ignorant, yet love bids me
> These farewell lines to recommend to thee,
> That when that knot's untied that made us one,
> I may seem thine, who in effect am none.

If she did perish, she said,

> The many faults that well you know I have,
> Let be interred in my oblivions grave;
> If any worth or virtue were in me,
> Let that live freshly in thy memory.[23]

Simon was away so frequently on governmental business that Anne composed poetic letters to express her longing for him. In "A Letter to her Husband, absent upon Publick employment" she referred to him as her life, her joy, her "Magazine of earthly store, / If two be one, as surely thou and I, / How stayest thou there, whilst I at Ipswich lie?" He was her sun, and in his absence her "chilled limbs now numbed lie forlorn." She viewed "those fruits which through thy heat I bore . . . / Which sweet contentment yield me for a space, / True living Pictures of their Father's face." A reference to Genesis 2:23 ended the work: "Flesh of thy flesh, bone of thy bone, / I here, thou there, yet both but one."[24]

She composed two poems bearing the same title, "Another." In the first, she portrayed herself as her husband's "widowed wife" beset by groans, tears, sobs, "longing hopes," and "doubting fears." After all, if he loved her, "how can he there abide?" In the second, she allowed her poetic imagery to take flight. She was the Hind and Simon was the Deer:

> As loving Hind that . . . wants her Deer,
> Scuds through the woods and Fern with harkening ear,
> Perplexed, in every bush & nook doth pry,
> Her dearest Deer, might answer ear or eye;
> So doth my anxious soul, which now doth miss,
> A dearer Dear (far dearer Heart) than this.
> Still wait with doubts, & hopes, and failing eye,
> His voice to hear, or person to descry.

While he was gone, she led "a joyless life" and had "a loving fear," yet "seemed no wife." She ended it: "Thy loving Love and Dearest Dear, / At home, abroad, and every where."[25]

Both parents, Grandmother and Grandfather Dudley, and the associated aunts and uncles had an eye on the future of the education of the Bradstreet children and the other children in the colony. The Puritans stressed the importance of education, and Samuel Eliot Morison noted that "learning was one of the by-products of English Puritanism that came over in the Winthrop fleet." He added, "Of all classes and elements in the English population, the puritans [*sic*] placed the highest value on learning." The churches required educated ministers to "interpret the sacred scriptures," and the congregations needed education to understand the sermons as well as the Scriptures.[26] Before 1646, about 130 alumni from Oxford, Cambridge, and Dublin lived in New England, and at least a third of them had arrived by 1638.[27] These immigrants wanted to make sure that their sons did not miss out on the educational advantages that they had in Old England by moving to New England.

The year after the Dudleys, Bradstreets, and Denisons moved to Ipswich, the General Court appropriated funds to set up a college. Another infusion of funds came from an unlikely source. Young John Harvard, a graduate of Emmanuel College, Cambridge, had received his master's degree in 1635, and he was living in Charlestown by 1637. Within the next year, he died of consumption, having left half his estate and a four-hundred-volume library to the college. The college was thus named for him, and it was established in the newly named Cambridge, formerly Newtowne.[28] Thomas Dudley served on the Board of Overseers of the college until his death.

Harvard College opened in 1638 with nine students and one master in a small house in the cow yard that had been owned by the town.[29] In its early years, students came from all New England colonies, England, Bermuda, and Virginia. The first scholarship fund for Harvard was created in 1643 by Ann Radcliffe, Lady Mowlson, a Puritan living in England. Radcliffe College, a college established for women—much later—and one of the Seven Sisters, was named for her. It merged with Harvard in the late twentieth century. Samuel Bradstreet, age five when the college opened, graduated from there in 1653, and his brother, Simon, graduated seven years later, much to the delight of their family. In 1665, the first Native American graduated from Harvard.

As the wilderness was being tamed and the young men of the colony gained a place to go for advanced learning, Anne kept writing poetry. Her undated poem "Contemplations," which was thirty-three stanzas long, has received the most critical acclaim over the centuries. The outer world of nature led her to reflect on her inner world and her Creator:

I wish not what to wish, yet sure thought I,
If so much excellence abide below;
How excellent is he that dwells on high?
Whose power and beauty by his works we know.

She thought of the "stately Oak" and the "glittering Sun," whose beams were "shaded by the leafy Tree." Then she thought of small creatures:

I heard the merry grasshopper then sing,
The black clad Cricket, bear a second part,
They kept one tune, and played on the same string,
Seeming to glory in their little Art.
Shall Creatures abject, thus their voices raise?
And in their kind resound their maker's praise:
Whilst I as mute, can warble forth no higher lays.

She brought up Adam and Eve, cast from Eden. Cain and Abel's sacrifices of "Fruits of the Earth, and Fatlings," were followed by Cain's "fratricide and "the Virgin Earth, of blood her first draught drinks." Then she reflected on man's immortality:

> Shall I then praise the heavens, the trees, the earth
> Because their beauty and their strength last longer
> Shall I wish there, or never to had birth,
> Because they're bigger, and their bodies stronger?
> Nay, they shall darken, perish, fade and die,
> And when unmade, so ever shall they lie,
> But man was made for endless immortality.

Sitting in "a lonely place" near the river and under the "shady woods," she mused on fish leaving their "numerous fry" in "lakes and ponds" and birds "warbling out" the old day. Turning again to man, she wrote:

> Man at the best a creature frail and vain,
> In knowledge ignorant, in strength but weak,
> Subject to sorrows, losses, sickness, pain,
> Each storm his state, his mind, his body break,
> From some of these he never finds cessation,
> But day or night, within, without, vexation,
> Troubles from foes, from friends, from dearest, nearest Relation.
>
> . . . .
>
> He that faileth in this world of pleasure,
> Feeding on sweets, that never bit of the sour,
> That's full of friends, of honour and treasure,
> Fond fool, he takes this earth even for heaven's bower.
> But sad affliction comes and makes him see

Here's neither honour, wealth, nor safety;
Only above is found all with security.
. . . .
But he whose name is graved in the white stone [See Rev. 2:17.]
Shall last and shine when all of these are gone.[30]

According to one critic, the poem expressed the "Puritan ideal of living fully in the world without being of it."[31] That was the balance for which Anne was always striving, whether in town or in the wilderness.

MISTRESS HUTCHINSON

Mistress Hutchinson, unlike Mistress Bradstreet, strayed far from Puritan ideals. The Massachusetts Bay Colony was rocked to its very foundations in 1637 when a legal case involving Anne Hutchinson, who came to be known as the American Jezebel, made its way to the General Court. The whole colony seemed to come to a stop to watch what was happening because its implications were so serious. John Winthrop was once again governor, and he and other leaders had been trying to keep the people safe from the threat of Native Americans and deal with other issues confronting them in the colony. They trod a new trail with this trial, however.

To better understand the situation, we need to understand the Puritans' view of a godly woman. We have a good example explicitly stated by Thomas Shepard, the pastor of the church in Newtowne (later called Cambridge), Massachusetts, who was another graduate of Emmanuel College, Cambridge. When he preached, he sought "to show the people their misery" and the remedy for them, Jesus Christ. His second wife, Joanna, died in childbirth after several years of marriage, and she left him two sons.

Shepard wrote about her in his memoirs and said that her death was a great loss to him because she was the comfort of his life. Joanna was his "most dear, precious, meek, and loving wife" with an "incomparable meekness of spirit." She had many wonderful traits:

> Of great prudence to take care for and order my family affairs, being neither too lavish nor sordid in anything. . . . She had an excellency to reprove for sin, and discern the evils of men. She loved God's people dearly, and [was] studious to profit by their fellowship, and therefore loved their company. She loved God's word exceedingly, and hence was glad she could read my notes, which she had to muse on every week. She had a spirit of prayer. . . . The last sacrament before her lying-in, seemed to be full of Christ, and thereby fitted for heaven.[1]

Then there was Mistress Hutchinson, who was anything but meek. She was born in England to a father who was an Anglican pastor and a mother who was related to the poet John Dryden. Her father, like Anne Bradstreet's, took special interest in his daughter's education, and among other topics, he instructed her in Scripture and theological dogma.[2] She married William Hutchinson, a merchant from Alford in Lincolnshire, about twenty miles north of Boston, England, and they had fifteen children, most born in England.

Anne and William were taken with the teachings of John

Cotton of St. Botolph's in Boston, England, and it is more than likely that they knew the Bradstreets and the Dudleys there and certainly after they came to New England. When John Cotton fled to Massachusetts, the Hutchinsons followed him and became citizens in Boston. William's success as a merchant brought him into a prominent position, and he was elected a member of the General Court for a time. Anne was known for her benevolent works, especially tending the sick and serving as a skilled midwife.

The problems began after Mistress Hutchinson started holding meetings for women twice a week in her home, and the group grew until more than eighty attended. Women instructing women in this way was not a new idea, but she took it to a new level. Initially she explained Cotton's message to attendees, but she eventually shared her views about his sermons, made what most ministers in the colony considered unorthodox comments about the Scriptures, and "meddled with theology" in her interpretation of the covenant of grace. She claimed to have "knowledge of the divine will from her own inner consciousness,"[3] as one historian put it. The complicated controversy was known as the antinomian controversy. John Winthrop wrote in his history: "One Mrs. Hutchinson, a member of the church of Boston, a woman of ready wit and bold spirit, brought over with her [from England] two dangerous errours: '1. That the person of the Holy Ghost dwells in a justified person. 2. That no sanctification can help to evidence to us our justification.'" Her presentations were so compelling that soon men started to attend the meetings with their wives, and because of her comments, many of those men did not fight in the Pequot War, much to the consternation of the governor.[4] *Hutchinsonians* was the term applied to her followers. Before the saga was over, Mistress Hutchinson was subjected to a civil trial and a religious trial.

Two men made known their scathing opinions of the woman who threatened the order in the colony. Rev. Thomas Weld said that Mistress Hutchinson was "of a haughty and fierce carriage, of a nimble wit and active spirit, and a very voluble tongue, more bold than a man, though in understanding and judgment inferior to many women."[5] John Winthrop was distressed about the discussions at her meetings and also the loss of productivity: "Many families were neglected and much time lost" because women were with her so often.[6] We have learned, from his description of his wife, what Rev. Shepard expected in a godly Puritan woman.

In early November 1637, Mistress Hutchinson was called before the General Court for a civil trial held at the meetinghouse in Newtowne. By all accounts, the room was full, but no record indicates that Anne Bradstreet was among the observers or that she left a comment about the proceedings. She had to know details of the trial because her husband and her father were involved.

John Winthrop presided. As the secretary, Simon Bradstreet recorded the events and was permitted to ask questions, and Thomas Dudley was another questioner. Eight ministers, including Thomas Shepard and Thomas Weld, testified against Mistress Hutchinson. Not only had she "troubled the peace of the commonwealth and the churches," but she was charged with "traducing the ministers and their ministry" and heresy.[7]

John Winthrop opened by saying to her, "You have spoken divers things, as we have been informed, very prejudicial to the honour of the churches and ministers thereof, and you have maintained a meeting and an assembly at your house that hath been condemned by the general assembly as a thing not tolerable nor comely in the sight of God nor fitting for your sex."[8] For a forty-six-year-old Puritan woman, who had just been at the birth of her first grandchild and was in the early stages of her own pregnancy, Mistress Hutchinson did not seem to be intimidated by him or the other men sitting in judgment of her. She stood before the court in her own defense, and she let her "nimble wit" fly.

Thomas Dudley's questions to her were harsher than those from Simon Bradstreet. Both men were strict adherents to the Puritan faith, but Bradstreet was more moderate than his father-in-law in confronting the accused and was a fierce advocate of freedom of speech. Bradstreet suggested to Mistress Hutchinson that she should discontinue her meetings "because they gave offence" and added that he was not against all women's meetings.[9]

In the give-and-take of the two-day trial, Mistress Hutchinson very nearly cleared herself of all charges against her. Then she made a critical and damning comment: she claimed to have direct revelations from God. To Puritans, "divine revelation closed with the Book of Revelation. Convicted out of her own mouth, Anne Hutchinson was sentenced to banishment from Massachusetts Bay 'as being a woman not fit for our society.'"[10] She was held under house arrest until her religious trial a few months later.

In 1637, an assembly of representatives of the Massachusetts churches had met in the first religious synod of the colony to define the accepted, orthodox views. The presiding official was Thomas Shepard. The synod condemned more than eighty "erroneous opinions" and several "unlawful practices."[11] That set the tone for Mistress Hutchinson's religious trial in late March 1638 at the First Church of Boston, with Rev. John Wilson presiding. She was deemed guilty of heresy and excommunicated.

The Hutchinsons and many Hutchinsonians left Massachusetts, and the Hutchinsons settled in Rhode Island, where Anne continued to hold meetings apart from the church. When Mistress Hutchinson miscarried her child at seven months and John Winthrop heard about it, he wrote, "See how the wisdom of God fitted this judgment to her sinne every way, for look as she had vented mishapen opinions, so she must bring forth deformed monsters."[12] After the death of her husband, Mistress Hutchinson and her seven younger children moved to Pelham Bay in New York. The fifty-one-year-old widow and all but one of those children were scalped or beheaded by Native Americans and placed in their house, and then all was set on fire. She had been warned of a possible raid, but she refused to keep firearms or leave the area.

More than three centuries passed before Anne Hutchinson's case was brought before another governmental body in Massachusetts, and the outcome was nothing like that of 1637. In 1945, the Massachusetts legislature revoked Anne Hutchinson's banishment, and in 1987, the governor pardoned her. Commissioned in 1920 by women's groups, a statue of her in front of the State House in Boston commends her as a "courageous exponent of civil liberty and religious toleration."[13]

LIBERTIES AND LOSSES

Anne Bradstreet's "life was proof . . . that creative art may be furthered by religion; and that even the duties of a housewife and mother in a new country cannot quench the sacred flame," wrote Samuel Eliot Morrison. "Her art was not an escape from life, but an expression of life."[1] Life was all around her in her growing brood of children, three under the age of five by 1638, and she had to care for them before she set pen to paper. Keeping everyone healthy and properly fed and starting to teach Samuel to read were just some of the items on her daily to-do list. Anne was fortunate that her children took after their father in having good health and being strong; they were seldom sick, but she still had to be prepared for the possibility.

In the seventeenth century, good health in body and mind was said to result from the correct balance of the four humors: blood (hot), phlegm (cold), yellow bile (dry), and black bile (moist). Too much blood made one fiery; too much phlegm, calm; too much yellow bile, bad tempered or choleric; and too much black bile, melancholic or despondent. Physicians and mothers relied on this system. In 1620, William Harvey learned about blood circulation, but even physicians were not yet sure what to do with that knowledge.[2]

A handful of doctors lived in Massachusetts Bay Colony, but for the most part, women in general and midwives in particular took care of the health needs of the colonists. Keeping the necessary herbs and other plants on hand was another never-ending task. Even Governor Winthrop offered health care advice. He recommended pills made from grated pepper and turpentine mixed with flour to treat a fever. He had this remedy for an infection: go outside, place several toads in a pot, set the pot on charcoal, and cook until done. Allow the pot to cool, take out the toads, and pound them in a mortar until they become powder. Mix the powder in liquid and drink it all down.

Some illnesses were the same as Anne and her mother had known in England, but others were new in New England. One of the most serious and common illnesses of New England children was what their parents referred to as a "griping of the belly" accompanied by fever and/or chills, followed by severe dysentery. Then there were colds, fevers of various kinds, influenza, worms, chin cough (whooping cough), and croup (the term used for laryngitis, diphtheria, or strep throat). Adults seemed prone to pleurisy, emphysema, kidney stones, gout, headaches, cancers, palsies, and dropsy (swelling associated with heart or kidney disease). Scrofula, a tubercular infection of lymph glands in the neck, affected both children and adults but was more common in children under the age of seven. Smallpox epidemics were sporadic, but from 1644 to 1649, outbreaks were almost constant in Massachusetts. Cholera was caused by contaminated water.

Maintaining sanitary conditions in even the best households was complicated by no running water or septic systems, and people bathed infrequently. Then there were accidents, serious and otherwise. Children were burned by fire or drowned in ponds. To the Puritans, God's hand was in everything that happened, including sickness, and fast days were often held during episodes of widespread illness.[3]

New England women had to learn about new plants and herbs that did not grow in Old England, and they sent for seeds or concoctions that they could not find in the New World. The Native Americans were helpful in providing plants or showing treatment methods, such as using alder bark on a cut or turpentine from pine on wounds.[4]

A few examples of conditions and cures are offered here *not* as recommendations to be followed by readers but as illustrations of the Puritans' medical limitations:

Chamomile: oil for pains and aches, especially in joints and kidney stone pain; boiled flowers for colds.

Cucumbers: juice applied to sunburn and freckles (freckles were undesirable, and the juice was supposed to lighten them).

Fennel: three drops of fennel oil a day for kidney stones.

Figwort: as a tonic for scrofula; as a poultice for burns or wounds.

Wild carrots: seeds for kidney stones; leaves applied with honey for running sores.

Wild mallows: leaves boiled down to oil applied to the area of "grief," for pleurisy.[5]

A serious illness, epilepsy (also known as falling sickness), called for more drastic measures than herbs. The ashes of the dung of a black cow were given to an infant to prevent him from having epilepsy or to cure it. Older people were offered livers of forty water frogs ground to a powder in spirit of rosemary or lavender five times a day; they were not to have food or drink for two hours before or after.[6]

Women's conditions had specific treatments. Drinking boiled pennyroyal "provoked women's courses." (*Pennyroyal* is a perennial herb in the mint genus, and its crushed leaves smell much like spearmint; the essential oil of pennyroyal is toxic if taken internally. Today it is used as a natural insect repellent.) Drinking wine with columbine seeds in it speeded the delivery of a child. Eating wild carrots aided in conception.[7] (After the long wait for her first child, Anne seemed to have no trouble conceiving seven more children.) The formula for a difficult labor was more complicated: start with a lock of hair from a virgin half the age of the woman in labor, and pound it into fine powder. Then take twelve ants' eggs dried in an oven and made into powder, and add that to the hair powder. Give the concoction with a pint of red cow's milk or in strong ale to the woman.[8]

Getting the proper nutrition was a way to help keep the four humors in balance and avoid having to follow some of the recommended "cures." By 1638, the colonists' diet improved significantly from what was available to them in 1630. Thriving vegetables and herbs included corn, cabbage, lettuce, thyme, sage, carrots, parsnips, red beets, radishes, turnips, wheat, peas, pennyroyal, rosemary, pumpkins, fennel, dill, coriander, and cucumbers. During the winter, people relied on smoked, salted, and pickled foods. Cheese and butter were common. In the better houses, meat such as beef, mutton, lamb, pork, ham, bacon, and smoked and dried fish were available. Cod was so prevalent that the colonists also exported it, and it was a significant source of revenue for them. They continued to hunt wild game: deer, ducks, geese, and doves. After the wild turkeys disappeared, they raised domestic ones. Spices and some nuts, such as nutmeg, pepper, cinnamon, English walnuts, and almonds, had to be imported. Lemons came from the Mediterranean or West Indies.[9]

Fruit was preserved and dried: apples, pears, cranberries, peaches, cherries, crab apples, and plums. In addition to being used in cooking, apples were the major component of cider. Some people brewed their own beer, and Robert Sedgwick established the first recorded brewery in the colony by 1637, but most beer was imported.[10] Wine had to be imported because the New England soil was not suitable for vineyards; Madeira proved to be a favorite.[11]

Like most Puritans, the Bradstreets usually ate three meals a day: breakfast, dinner (which was the main meal at midday), and a light supper in the evening. That meant the fire in the fireplace was going all the time because everything was cooked from scratch. (Cheese and soap and dipped candles were also made in the large kettles, not at the same time, of course.) Many foods were boiled: stews, soups, and porridge. Porridge was the typical breakfast food, sometimes made of boiled milk with cornmeal and sometimes just bean porridge. Baking in the Bradstreet household was reserved for one day a week, using a brick oven built into the chimney. On Saturday, Anne cooked the brown bread and baked beans for meals on Sunday because Puritans did not work on Sunday. She or her servants roasted meat on a spit near the open fire.[12]

As Simon, Anne, and the children gathered for a meal, their tableware, which consisted of dishes and trenchers (platters), was made of pewter or wood. In most Bay Colony households, wooden spoons and trenchers were common, no matter what one's measure of wealth. Because of its cost and its care, having pewterware indicated that a family was better off. Pewterware required much polishing to keep shiny, and that task was done by servants. Many colonists brought pewter with them from England, and others bought it as they could afford it. Table forks of the colonial era had only two tines, and Governor Winthrop may have had the first one in the New World. Forks were rare even in England in the 1630s. The Bradstreet children ate with spoons, made of wood or pewter, and their fingers. Two children might have shared one wooden trencher, or each might have had his or her own wooden bowl. Anne and Simon used a knife and spoon and their fingers on the cod and roasted carrots and parsnips served on pewter plates. All used napkins. Anne and the children probably had pewter drinking cups, and Simon could have had a stoneware jug (like a tankard). It is possible that the family owned a silver spoon or two, but silverware was rare at that stage of colonial history.[13]

Most food was cooked in a simple way, but as Anne and Simon became better off and as they entertained more, Anne probably branched out into more elaborate preparation. John Murrell released his *New Book of Cookerie* in 1615, which contained receipts (recipes) for the "newest and most commendable fashion of dressing, boiling, saucing, or roasting, all manner either flesh, fish, or any kind of fowl."[14] It was so popular that a fifth edition was released in 1638. Although we do not know whether Anne or her mother or neighbors had a copy of the book, they likely knew how to do this kind of cooking. There were instructions for boiling a capon larded with lemons, a leg of mutton, pigeons with rice, rabbits with herbs, and sparrows; for baking eels, chickens with grapes, deer, sheep's tongues, wild boar, swan, geese, gooseberry tart, cherry tart, and oyster pie; for saucing oysters, carp, and pigs; and for making puddings from veal or goose.

Recipes then left a lot to be desired in terms of measurements and precise instructions. How could Anne know that the fire in her fireplace was the appropriate temperature for saucing carp? Her cooking depended on experience and educated guesswork. Murrell's recipe for Cambridge pudding, given below, provides an example of the cooking instructions. Most puddings were not creamy but were either solid or soft and spongy. The term could refer to a savory dish, such as black pudding (boiled pig blood mixed with pork fat and spices), but a pudding was usually a dessert, such as rice pudding or this one:

Cambridge Pudding
Grate bread, and mince it with flour, dates, currants,
    nutmeg, cinnamon, pepper, and suet.
Add warm milk, fine sugar, and eggs but do not include
    all whites.
Work it together, and make it round like a loaf.
Put butter in the middle of the pudding.
Boil liquor, and put the pudding, tied in a cloth, into that.

Boil it "enough."
Cut and serve it.[15]

In addition to cooking, Anne oversaw the care of the livestock, especially when Simon was away, as well as making candles and soap, sewing towels and bed linens, and repairing and cleaning clothing. Most of the colonists' clothing was imported in the early days, but eventually Anne and the other women were responsible for spinning, weaving, and making clothing of wool or flax. Anne probably did not do most of this work herself because she had men and women servants. She started overseeing Samuel's chores too. Even young children had chores, such as weeding gardens or picking berries. As boys got older, they gathered wood and fetched water, and as girls got older, they sewed or knitted simple items such as stockings or did household chores.[16]

Teaching her children to read and write was another of Anne's duties, one that she probably enjoyed since she was such an avid student. One scholar believes that much of her poetry was a teaching aid for her children and perhaps her nieces and nephews, and that may be one reason she wrote it in the first place.[17] (See especially her long poems, "The Four Elements," "The Four Humours," "The Four Ages of Man," and "The Four Seasons of the Year" in chapter 11.)

Amid all this, Anne was writing poetry in her "spare" time, like this one about Sir Philip Sidney, courtier to Queen Elizabeth, diplomat, poet, patron of poets, and soldier. She called it "An Elegie upon that Honourable and renowned Knight Sir Philip Sidney, who was untimely slain at the Siege of Zutphen, Anno, 1586." He and other English soldiers were fighting with the

Dutch against Spain when he was killed. His works, poetry and prose, were published posthumously, and he is known especially for the collection of sonnets *Astrophel and Stella*. Many English poets wrote works praising him, and that might have been one reason for Anne to write this elegy. It was also an opportunity to praise Queen Elizabeth:

> When England did enjoy her halcyon days,
> Her noble Sidney wore the Crown of Bays;
> As well an honour to our British Land,
> As she that swayed the Scepter with her hand.[18]

"The brave refiner of our British tongue," Sidney was eloquent, logical, witty, and musical in his poetry, and his critics were "Beetle-heads." (Beetle-heads are stupid people. In Shakespeare's *Taming of the Shrew*, Petruchio called another character a "beetle-headed, flap-ear'd knave."[19]) Anne praised Sidney's learning, valor, morality, and sense of justice. She was unsure whether her Muse could do him justice, but "Sidney's Muse can sing his worthiness." He was "Heir to the Muses, the Son of Mars in Truth."

In this poem from 1638, she wrote that she had the "self-same blood yet in my veins" as in Sidney's veins. Years later, she revised it to "English blood yet runs within my veins." Sidney's mother was a Dudley, and although her father was convinced of the family kinship with Sidney, perhaps Anne became less certain of it.[20]

Once again elected deputy governor, Thomas Dudley chose to make his final move in Massachusetts. He and Dorothy went to Roxbury, a few miles southwest of Boston. This time Anne and Simon and the other Dudley children did not accompany their parents. Anne and Simon remained in Ipswich for the time being, and that was the farthest Anne had been from her parents since they came to New England. The Dudleys had five or six acres, and once more they became the prominent family in town. Deputy Governor Dudley built a substantial home with two parlors, a parlor chamber, a hall chamber, a study, and other rooms. The house stood until it was razed after the Battle of Bunker Hill at the outset of the American Revolution in 1775.[21]

The year 1640 was one of momentous events for the Dudleys and Bradstreets, for the colony, and for England. Anne had her second son, named after her husband; the first printer in Massachusetts printed the first book in America; and King Charles I convened Parliament for the first time in years so that he could raise money to fight the Scots opposing his policies related to the church.

Stephen Daye established his printing business in Cambridge in 1639 and printed the oath for freemen. The next year he had a much bigger project when he printed seventeen hundred copies of *The Whole Booke of Psalmes Faithfully Translated into English Metre* (usually abbreviated as the *Bay Psalm Book*). John Eliot was one of the ministers who worked on the manuscript. The singing of entire psalms, not in paraphrased form, was important to Puritans, and they used this book in church and at home. Here is the wording of the first part of Psalm 23:

> The Lord to mee a shepheard is,
> want therefore shall not I,
> Hee in the folds of tender-grasse,
> doth cause mee down to lie.

The Old South Church in Boston now owns two original copies of the book.[22]

Old England had been having more than its share of troubles on the home front and had left Massachusetts Bay Colony to its own devices after failing to take back the charter. King Charles I and Archbishop Laud were faced with developments that removed them as threats to the colony. They were unprepared for the resistance from the members of Parliament who had had plenty of time to think about their grievances against the king. Then an added problem arose with the division of Puritans and Anglicans, and before all of them knew it, they were in the midst of a civil war by 1642. The Roundheads opposed the king and consisted of Puritans, militant members of Parliament, merchants, and most people from southern and eastern England. The Cavaliers supported the king and consisted of Catholics, nobles, about half of Parliament, and most people from northern and western England. The war lasted seven long years.

The earless Puritan William Prynne was finally released from prison in 1640 when the king started to lose his powers, and Parliament impeached Archbishop Laud for high treason, among other crimes, and imprisoned him in the Tower of London. When Laud's trial was finally held in 1644, William Prynne led the prosecution against Laud but could not prove treason. Determined to get rid of the archbishop, both houses of Parliament issued a special decree to condemn him, and Laud was beheaded early in 1645, a vivid foreshadowing of what awaited the king.

By 1640, about twenty-six thousand immigrants had come to New England during the Great Migration. A piece of trivia that is not so trivial is that two and a half centuries later, the

United States had a population of about 20 million people, and one-quarter of them sprang from those New Englanders.[23] With the changes that began in England in 1640, fewer immigrants, Puritans or otherwise, arrived in the Massachusetts Bay Colony because they were so hopeful about improvements for them in their homeland. They also felt an obligation to do their part if they were needed to participate in the revolution. That meant fewer new homes to be built and fewer new people to buy goods in Massachusetts. The governmental uncertainty in England made trade relations almost impossible for the New Englanders. Colonial commodities brought low prices, and the colonists scrambled to pay their debts in England. European commodities became scarce in the colony too.

The uproar affecting English law and lawmakers is in sharp contrast to the measured efforts at creating law in Massachusetts Bay Colony in the same time frame. Several people had input into the process that had begun in 1638, but the primary creators of the Body of Liberties were John Winthrop, John Cotton, and Nathaniel Ward. Ward, the neighbor of the Bradstreets and their former pastor in Ipswich, is credited with the final product that the General Court accepted. While in England, he had studied law and practiced for ten years in London, so the Body of Liberties has a firm basis in English common law.[24]

The Body of Liberties[25] applied to all people in the colony, whether citizens or otherwise. It covered courts, jury duty, property, and wills and estates. Not only were the rights of free men set forth, but women were granted two specific rights. One concerned being left a "competent portion" of a dead husband's estate, and the other stated plainly: "Every married woman shall be free from bodily correction or stripes [that is, being whipped] by her husband, unless it be in his own defense upon her assault." According to English common law, a man could use a "reasonable instrument" on his wife. The liberties of children discussed what to do with minor children upon the deaths of parents and the recourse of children if their parents were unnecessarily severe with them. Animal cruelty was forbidden.

Theft was not a capital crime in Massachusetts, but it was in England if the stolen item was worth more than a designated amount. Capital offenses included worship of idols, witchcraft, blasphemy, premeditated murder, adultery, sedition, and perjury. (Adultery, blasphemy, and perjury were not capital offenses in England.) Two adulterers were executed in Boston in 1644; however, the death penalty for blasphemy or perjury was never noted in the colonial records.

Another section dealt with the liberties that the Lord Jesus gave to the churches. That included holding private meetings "for edification in religion amongst Christians of all sorts of people," as long as they were without "just offense for number, time, place, and other circumstances."

The colonists were not satisfied with these laws, though, and within a few years they tackled the subject again. They built on the Body of Liberties[26] and added general laws to create Laws and Liberties, which dealt with crime, property rights, trade, governmental affairs, military operations, and the relations of church and state. They dealt with idleness, for which the offender could be brought before the court and punishment would be handed out as the members thought "meet to inflict." Each township was to care for the poor within its boundaries, and fines and penalties could be imposed for letting one's pigs invade a neighbor's pastures or corn or gardens.

Capital offenses included idolatry, witchcraft, blasphemy, bestiality, adultery, rape, man stealing (that is, kidnapping Africans—instead of buying them—to then sell into slavery), treason, false witness with intent to take life, smiting a parent (applied to a son over the age of sixteen), and homicide. Due process of law was to be carried out for all.

In January 1642, due process in England gave way to martial solutions when King Charles and his men attempted to arrest five of his most vocal critics in the House of Commons. The five escaped before the king arrived, and Charles was confronted by forces of the City of London and had to flee the city. By August, he had enough forces of his own to declare war on Parliament. When John Winthrop heard about what happened in England, he encouraged the General Court to maintain the neutrality of Massachusetts Bay during the conflict.

Anne felt so strongly about the events unfolding in England that she wrote "A Dialogue between Old England and New; concerning their present Troubles, Anno, 1642."[27] She portrayed Old England as the mother and New England as the child. New England started by asking Old England, "Dear Mother, fairest Queen," what ailed her. Old England responded that she had woes and griefs and stated their cause:

> My sins the breach of sacred Laws,
> Idolatry supplanter of a Nation,
> With foolish Superstitious Adoration,
> Are liked and countenanced by men of might,

The Gospel trodden down and hath no right:
Church Offices were sold and bought for gain.

The upshot was that the pope hoped to find Rome in England. Sabbath breakers and drunkenness were too common in Old England, and "Princely heads on blocks [were] laid down / For naught but title to a fading crown."

New England agreed that there were many "fearful sins" to lament in Old England and asked about the "present grief." The issue was the "Question of State" between the king and the peers, said Old England, that is, "Which is the chief, the Law, or else the King." There was much contention between the subjects and the king.

New England sympathized: "Your griefs I pity, but soon hope to see, / Out of your troubles much good fruit to be." She recalled earlier times:

After dark Popery the day did clear,
But now the Sun in his brightness shall appear. . . .
These are the days the Churches foes to crush
To root out Popelings head, tail, branch, and rush.

New England was hopeful that laws, truth, and righteousness would triumph and the "happy Nation" would again flourish: "Farewell dear Mother, rightest cause prevail, / And in a while, you'll tell another tale."[28]

Anne wrote poetry in response to the events in England, but the New England leaders in 1643 formed a confederation of United Colonies—Plymouth, New Haven, Connecticut, and

Massachusetts—and drew up the Articles of Confederation. The onset of the civil war placed New England on alert for "foreign and domestic enemies," especially the Royalists who might want to force them to be subject to the king's authority. Then there were the French on the east, the Dutch on the west, and Native Americans all around. The General Court in Massachusetts took action to ensure that the colony would have necessary items for defense, and the court ordered a fast "as a day of public humiliation . . . in regard of our own straits, and the foul sins broken out amongst us, and the distractions of our native country, Ireland, Holland, and the other parts of Europe."[29]

The poem "In Honour of that High and Mighty Princess Queen Elizabeth of Happy Memory" was a "tribute of a loyal brain" and expressed Anne's wishful thinking about just the woman who could resolve the troubles in England. Good Queen Bess had overcome multiple problems facing the country and had made it stronger and prosperous. Besides Anne's reading about the queen, her father had been in the queen's service and likely had positive stories to tell about her leadership. The queen's father furthered her education, just as Anne's father had furthered hers. Henry VIII early on discerned his daughter Elizabeth's intellect and made sure that she had the best education. She could speak Latin, Greek, French, and Italian. She learned theology, she committed to memory portions of the Old and New Testaments, and she brought them into discussions when appropriate. She read the classics by Cicero, Pliny, Seneca, Plato, and Aristotle, and she translated a dialogue of Xenophon into English. She wrote many speeches and poems.

She understood how affairs of state worked and how human beings could betray her and how they could support her.[30]

Anne made a point about how a woman could triumph, despite obstacles: "So great's thy glory and thine excellence . . . / That men account it no impiety, / To say thou wert a fleshly Deity."

The queen had the world as the "Theatre where she did act." In her "happy reign: / Who was so good, so just, so learned, so wise / From all the Kings on earth she won the prize." She "wiped off the aspersion of her Sex, / That women wisdom lack to play the Rex [ruler]." Elizabeth taught "better manners" to Spain's monarch when the English defeated the Spanish armada. Anne asked, "Was ever people better ruled than hers? . . . Did ever wealth in England more abound?" And some of that wealth was Spanish gold, brought home to the queen by Sir Francis Drake, whom she encouraged in his exploits.

Elizabeth had so many accomplishments that Anne could not tell half of them. There had been other queens,

> Yet for our Queen is no fit Parallel.
> Now say, have women worth? or have they none?
> Or had they some, but with our Queen is it gone?
> Nay Masculines, you have thus taxed us long,
> But she, though dead, will vindicate our wrong.
> Let such as say our Sex is void of Reason,
> Know 'tis a Slander now, but once was Treason.[31]

Anne had occasion to write another poem about another beloved woman and role model in 1643. Her mother died suddenly on December 27 at age sixty-one, most likely from a heart attack. Dorothy and Thomas had been married forty years, and most of what we know about Dorothy's personality comes from Anne's description in "An Epitaph on my dear and ever honoured Mother Mrs. Dorothy Dudley." She was a "Worthy Matron of unspotted life," a loving mother, an obedient wife, a "friendly Neighbor," and a friend of the poor, who provided them with clothing and food. To servants, she was "wisely awful, but yet kind." To the family, she was an instructor. She frequently attended public meetings, that is, lectures and sermons in the meetinghouse, and was "Religious in all her words and ways." Dorothy Dudley left a "blessed memory" at her death.[32]

By April of the next year, sixty-eight-year-old Thomas Dudley had married a widow who lived in Roxbury. Finding a new wife so quickly might have seemed disrespectful to the memory of Dorothy, but usually when a spouse died during that era, the widow or widower remarried within months. It came down to the practical matter of maintaining a household. Within a year of the marriage, Thomas had another daughter, Deborah, and he and his new wife also had two sons, Joseph, born in 1647, who followed in his father's steps and became governor of Massachusetts, and Paul, born in 1650.

Soon after her mother's death and her father's remarriage, the changes just kept coming for Anne. Simon had made up his mind that Andover, yet another wilderness area, was the place for them. When thirty-two-year-old Anne left Ipswich, it was as if she left her Muse of lofty poetry behind. Her poetry from that point forward was less ambitious in length and subject, but the poems that survive are the most personal ones she composed.

ANDOVER

ndover was about sixteen miles farther inland than
Ipswich and twenty miles or so directly north of Boston.
The area in which Anne and Simon and their family
established themselves is in present-day North Andover. Anne
must have felt some consolation in her new surroundings because
her sister Mercy and her family had preceded them. Yet Anne must
have also felt that they were starting all over again because there
were so few families in Andover. Andover would have seemed
deserted after being among the more than eight hundred residents of Ipswich, then the second largest town in the colony after
Boston.[1] And Anne had become used to stimulating discussions
with her learned neighbors and the companionship of her sister
Patience and the protection of her brother-in-law Daniel.[2]

Mercy became the bride of John Woodbridge in 1639, and
they lived in Newbury, where John was the town clerk and then
served as deputy to the General Court. He was the leader of
a group from Ipswich and Newbury that settled in Andover in
1641. By then, he and Mercy had two daughters, Sarah and Lucy.

A letter from Thomas Dudley to his son-in-law John changed the course of John's life. In the letter, Thomas encouraged John to become a teacher or minister because Thomas did not think the young man had the nature for a planter: "Every man ought (as I take it) to serve God in such a way whereto he had best filled him by nature, education or gifts, or graces required."[3] John took his father-in-law's advice and was ordained the minister of Andover, and a meetinghouse was built there.

The Bradstreets did not move until 1644, two years before the incorporation of Andover, but Simon soon became the most distinguished citizen and biggest property owner. He was determined to work hard and make his funds work hard too. Perhaps he had been inspired by the example of his father-in-law and mentor. He owned five hundred acres in Salem and more land in Topsfield, Watertown, Cambridge, and Boston; he built the first sawmill in Andover; and he owned saltworks at Nahant and ironworks in what is now Boxford.[4] He also had his governmental work.

With his comfortable income, Simon was able to build a nice home for Anne and the children, better than the one in Ipswich. The house, which some called a mansion, was set among green hillsides on Haverhill and Boston Roads. It had two stories in front but one in the back; its doors were small and low, and the interior had paneling with imported windows.

The Bradstreets had many worldly goods compared to most citizens, but it was a short list at that. They had beds (maybe feather) and linens and quilts, some books, basic furniture, and cooking wares. As their livelihood improved, they acquired silver and china to use on formal occasions. John Hull was a silversmith in Boston who made silver tankards, candlesticks, and platters, and they probably called upon his expertise.[5] Gradually they acquired fine furniture from England.

Just after they moved to Andover, Anne and Simon added to the family in 1645 with a daughter named Mercy after Anne's sister. The two boys and four girls ranged in age from twelve years to a few weeks. As the children learned to talk, they picked up forms of speech from their parents, aunts and uncles, and neighbors, all born in England. As another example of the enduring impact of these people on New England, the forms of speech they brought with them remained in use in New England long after those forms ceased to be common in Old England.

Anne made certain that her youngsters were able to read and write as soon as they could, but the General Court wanted to assure that other children in the colony shared that advantage. An act passed in 1642 made the education of children the responsibility of parents, who taught the children the three Rs at home. Within five years, the court passed an education act directed at communities, and fines were meted out for failure to comply. These two acts were significant in the development of public schools in America. Towns of fifty households were to have a schoolmaster to teach children to read because "one chief project of ye ould deluder, Satan, [was] to keep men from the knowledge of ye Scriptures."[6] Anne agreed with this sentiment, and she called Satan the "great Angler" who has bait to match the "tempers of men" and they perceive the hook "too late."[7] With the knowledge of the Scriptures, they could more readily perceive the hook. In towns of one hundred households, there was to be a grammar school to prepare boys (and note that it was for boys only) for college. The court held that the boys should learn to write, read, and speak well so they could communicate as good citizens and businessmen, to do their sums so they could conduct business efficiently, and to understand Latin and Greek so that the great literature would be accessible to them.

Some towns had taken the educational initiative before the passage of the second act. Boston Latin, founded in 1635, was modeled after the Free Grammar School in Boston, England; and Charlestown, Cambridge, and Roxbury set up schools before 1647. Boys started at age six or eight and studied at these schools for six years.[8] Dame schools developed for young children (boys and girls often as young as three) in homes of women. They were somewhat like neighborhood nursery schools, but the children did learn to read a primer or hornbook. The Bradstreet boys were taught by at least two schoolmasters, who were also ministers, in Andover; the first was their uncle John Woodbridge, and the second was Francis Dane.

Anne's ability to manage the younger children's education and keep the household running smoothly was well known among family and friends. But even she had run-ins with servants. Their servants accompanied them from Ipswich to Andover because servants—good ones or mediocre ones—were increasingly hard to find. Most servants preferred to work in the more established towns than on the edge of the wilderness. One maid so tried Anne's patience that Anne became angry with her, and the neighbors talked about it for several days. Anne, who erred on the kind side, was likely still honing skills learned from her mother to be "wisely awful, but yet kind" to servants. Later on, Anne did not tolerate the behavior of a manservant who stole food from the family, and the Bradstreets took him to court over the theft.

Somehow Anne managed to extend hospitality to guests with her less-than-adequate staff, and with Simon's increasing prosperity, they were able to serve feasts. Biographer Helen Campbell observed, "There are many hints that Mistress Bradstreet provided good cheer with a freedom born of her early training, and made stronger by her husband's tastes and wishes."[9] Many women in Andover followed her example.

Anne's sister Sarah—the sister after whom Anne named her third child—likely did not follow Anne's upstanding example, however.[10] At the very least, she appeared to have stepped firmly beyond the bounds of acceptable behavior for a Puritan woman. Sarah married Benjamin Keayne of Boston in 1638 when she was eighteen years old, and they had one child, Hannah. Things began to fall apart for Sarah in 1645 when Benjamin deserted her and sailed for England, perhaps because he owed money to creditors in New England. Sarah managed to accumulate what money she could (perhaps from the sale of property) to take to him in England, but she lost everything at sea. She barely escaped with her life on the treacherous voyage.

She was in London in mid-1646, but Benjamin refused to have anything to do with her. (It is not clear where the daughter, Hannah, was through all of this, but she was probably with the Keayne grandparents.) What is more, Benjamin wrote scathing, searing letters in March of that year to Sarah's father and to Rev. John Cotton and Rev. John Wilson. To the ministers, Benjamin accused Sarah of being unfaithful to him and claimed that she had "impoysoned" him with a venereal disease because he had not been with another woman. In the letter to Thomas Dudley, he stated, "I do plainly declare my resolution, never again to live with her as a husband."[11] He remained in England, but Sarah returned to Boston.

In November 1646, the church in Boston accused Sarah of "irregular prophesying in mixed assemblies" and of engaging in "unclean behavior" with a man who had been excommunicated from the church, and she too was excommunicated.[12] The extended Dudley family must have thought about the fate of Anne Hutchinson when one of their own was in obvious distress. How much worse would it get?

The next year, the General Court granted Sarah a divorce. The usual grounds for divorce at that time were desertion or adultery,[13] but if the court thought that she was guilty of adultery, she would have been subject to the penalty for that crime and would not have received the divorce. She did, however, lose custody of Hannah, and the paternal grandparents were the likely custodians. Hannah's paternal grandfather wrote in his will that Hannah's mother should not benefit from anything that he left to Hannah, and he referred to Sarah as the former "unnatural & unhappy wife of my son, that proud & disobedient daughter-in-law to myself & wife."[14]

Sarah's plight had to be the subject of much disapproving discussion in many homes since she was the daughter of such a prominent, upstanding man in the colony. For his part, Thomas Dudley helped her obtain a home in Roxbury, where she lived until she married Thomas Pacey of Boston in 1649. At some point, they separated because Sarah (then Mistress Pacey) was living alone in Boston. The town fathers permitted her to remain in the city only if Simon Bradstreet or one or two other men stood as security for her, meaning they made sure that the city would not have to support her as an indigent. Sarah died in Boston at age thirty-nine with ten pounds to her name, six years after her father's death.[15]

Essentially, Anne lost two sisters in 1647, but the causes were much different. When Sarah's case regarding her divorce went to the General Court, her sister Mercy's family was preparing to make a trip to England. The Massachusetts Bay Colony was officially neutral in the civil war, but most colonists were sympathetic to the Roundheads. Nevertheless, the colonists remained wary of both sides, and Simon Bradstreet became a commissioner of the United Colonies of New England, which endeavored to keep the colonists safe. There were then thirty-three settled towns in Massachusetts that required protection.[16]

John Woodbridge was taking Mercy and their four children with him to England, where he was to be the chaplain to the parliamentary commissioners trying to negotiate a treaty with the king to end the civil war. Fifteen commissioners from both houses of Parliament participated. Negotiations failed in late 1648, and the king was placed under arrest by the army in preparation for his trial, which was held in early 1649. Charles I was tried for treason, found guilty, and sentenced to death. He was beheaded on January 30, 1649, and Parliament abolished the monarchy and took over the government of the Commonwealth of England. What followed was a series of battles with Charles II, who refused to accept the abolition of the monarchy, and the Protectorate was established first under the Puritan Oliver Cromwell and then under his son, Richard Cromwell. The Protectorate ended with Richard Cromwell's resignation, and King Charles II was restored to the throne in mid-1660.

The Woodbridges remained in England until after the Restoration; John had spent the years serving as a minister. The family, which had grown by several children, returned to New England in 1663, too late to see their beloved Anne alive again. But John Woodbridge had succeeded in a historic achievement for his poetic sister-in-law in her thirty-eighth year: the publication of *The Tenth Muse Lately Sprung Up in America*.[17] And what a surprise for Anne!

THE TENTH MUSE
LATELY SPRUNG UP
IN AMERICA

When John Woodbridge and his family sailed for England in 1647, Woodbridge had Anne's manuscript of poems carefully protected and packed among their belongings. Debate has been ongoing since then, among biographers, historians, and literary critics, about whether he took the manuscript without Anne's knowledge and permission, but that is not the major point here. The point is that he managed to get a Puritan woman's poetry, written in New England, published by a well-known publisher in England in 1650. Granted, it took awhile, but it happened. Woodbridge must have been convinced of the worth of Anne's work, or he would not have made the attempt at publication in the first place, and acting like a combined agent and public relations representative, he had the assistance of several significant men to shepherd the process along and commend the work. Their praise at the beginning of her book was similar to modern-day book endorsements by respected public figures.

In order to have the rights to produce a legal printed work in England, one had to pay a fee and enter the title in the Stationers' Register. That was the record of the Stationers' Company in London, a trade guild to regulate the publishing industry; the process was much like the American process of obtaining a copyright. The publisher was Stephen Bowtell at the sign of the Bible in Pope's Head Alley, where he had his bookstore. The alley, named for the Pope's Head Tavern, was off Lombard Street in the City of London (the main business and governmental district).

Bowtell sold books, sermons, and religious pamphlets, and he published an unusual work by Anne's former pastor and neighbor, Nathaniel Ward, in 1647. It was *The Simple Cobler of Aggawam in America*, written while he was in New England. Ward had returned to England from Ipswich to live out the rest of his years in England. *The Simple Cobler* was a witty, satirical work denouncing all manner of Ward's dislikes and his view of the faults of both England and New England. Not only was it likely that Ward recommended Anne's manuscript to Bowtell, but he also commended her in a short poem included in the introductory material of her book and wrote, in part,

> It half revives my chill frost-bitten blood,
> To see a Woman once, do ought that's good;
> And chode by Chaucer's Boots, and Homer's Furrs,
> Let Men look to it, lest Women wear the Spurrs.[1]

His view of Anne was quite different from his attitude toward many women in the Massachusetts Bay Colony. After he condemned them for being overly concerned with fashions, he wrote in *The Simple Cobler*, "It is no marvel they wear drailes on the hinder part of their heads, having nothing as it seems in the fore-part, but a few Squirrel's brains to help them frisk from one ill-favoured fashion to another."[2] (Drailes are fishhooks and lines.) Clearly Anne did not fall into the squirrel-brained category.

The 1650 edition of Anne's poems filled 207 pages, and the title page read, *The Tenth Muse Lately Sprung Up in America, or Severall Poems, compiled with great variety of wit and learning, full of delight . . . by a Gentlewoman of those parts*. Her name did not appear on the title page but was included in the complimentary comments and poems written by the notable gentlemen. There were two other major editions of her work before the nineteenth century: the second edition in 1678 was printed in Boston by John Foster, and it contained her additions and corrections and some poems found after her death; the third edition was printed in Boston in 1758. Prose pieces found in Anne's small manuscript book, which had been held by her descendants, were published in *The Works of Anne Bradstreet in Prose and Verse*, edited by John Harvard Ellis in 1867. (Quotations from Anne's prose and verse in this book are from Ellis's edition of *Works*.)

John Woodbridge wrote the preface for the 1650 edition, and he first addressed the reader's possible disbelief that the author of the poems was a woman. He confirmed that the author was indeed a woman "honoured and esteemed" where she lived, "for her gracious demeanour, her eminent parts, her pious conversation, her courteous disposition, her exact diligence in her place, and discreet managing of her Family occasions." He made sure that everyone knew she was not neglecting her family to pore over pages of her poetry: "These Poems are the fruit but of some few hours, curtailed from her sleep and other refreshments." He stated that he "presumed to bring to public view" the poems without the knowledge of the author and "contrary to her expectation."[3] (The last lines started the long-running debate: Did she or did she not know he had her poems and intended to publish them? As a Puritan woman, she really should not have been publishing anything anyway.)

Benjamin Woodbridge, brother of John, was a minister, a graduate of Harvard College, and a short-term citizen of Andover before he returned to his native England. He wrote about Anne:

> Now I believe Tradition, which doth call
> The Muses, Virtues, Graces, Females all;
> Only they are not nine, eleven nor three;
> Our Authoress proves them but one unity.[4]

John Rogers was the son of Nathaniel Rogers of Ipswich, and he married Elizabeth Denison, the only daughter of Anne's sister Patience, so he was in the family. He was a minister and a medical doctor, and he served as president of Harvard College. His poetic comments, in nine stanzas, were included in the second edition of Anne's poems. He might have gone just a wee bit over the top in praise of her: "Twice have I drunk the Nectar of your lines"; "Your head the source [of the poems], whence all those springs did flow." Then he ended, "Here 'tis your name

/ Shall stand immarbled; this your little frame / Shall great Colossus be, to your eternal fame."[5]

Other men wrote in the same vein. It is hard not to compare the treatment of Anne Bradstreet to that of Anne Hutchinson as women doing things outside the usual sphere of the woman's world then. One was praised and the other banished. An early biographer of Anne Bradstreet, Luther Caldwell, may have hit on an explanation for the difference: "According to many able and learned men of her time, she was the most remarkable, level-headed and self-poised intellectual woman of the early colonial times," and she was "of the loftiest Puritan faith."[6]

Level-headed Anne used the prologue of the second edition to address critics of her and her work that she knew would arise. She was gracious but firm, and she was self-deprecating:

> To sing of Wars, of Captains, and Kings,
> Of Cities founded, Common-wealths begun,
> For my mean pen are too superiour things: . . .
> My obscure Lines shall not so dim their worth.

She defended her "Poet's pen":

> I am obnoxious to each carping tongue
> Who says my hand a needle better fits,
> A Poet's pen all scorn I should thus wrong;
> For such despite they cast on Female wits:
> If what I do prove well, it won't advance,
> They'll say it's stolen, or else it was by chance.

And she asked for fair treatment as a woman:

Let Greeks be Greeks, and women what they are
Men have precedency and still excel,
It is but vain unjustly to wage war;
Men can do best, and women know it well
Preeminence in all and each is yours;
Yet grant some small acknowledgment of ours.

She did not desire a laurel wreath, which was used in ancient Greece to honor or praise someone's accomplishment. Rather, a wreath of everyday thyme or parsley would be adequate for her.[7]

To prepare for composing her long poems, all of which were ambitious projects, Anne had to read and understand science, history, the Bible, and literature. She also had her keen eye on the nature surrounding her and on the political wranglings in both Massachusetts and England. A nineteenth-century critic commented on her "frequent and accurate allusions to ancient literature and to facts in history."[8] She dealt with everything from the mundane (bread made from barley and rye had "not so white a face" as wheat bread) to the sublime ("Here's neither honour, wealth, nor safety; / Only above is found all with security").[9]

The *Tenth Muse* begins with "The Four Elements," "Of the Four Humours in Man's Constitution," "The Four Ages of Man," and "The Four Seasons of the Year." Each of these four long poems had four sections. Nineteenth-century editor John Harvard Ellis considered the four long poems to be four parts of one exceedingly long poem. These poems could cause one to agree with the literary critic who believed Anne wrote them to instruct her children, especially since each had a religious or moral component.

"The Four Elements" is a conversation of fire, air, earth, and water as they "did contest / Which was the strongest, noblest and the best."

Fire was useful for cooking food, refining silver, providing warmth in homes, and making weapons, and of course, the heat of the sun was good for all living things. But there was a downside to fire: "And though I be a servant to each man / Yet by my force, master, my masters can. / What famous Towns, to Cinders have I turn'd?" Fire ended by saying, "In a word, the world I shall consume / And all therein, at that great day of Doom."

Earth talked of producing vineyards, gardens, orchards, and cornfields. Roots and herbs came from the earth to produce medicines. Mariners' ships and oars came from wood, and greedy miners dug for gold. Earth stated, "If ought you have, to use, to wear, to eat, / But what I freely yield, upon your sweat?" Despite his "toiling pain," man sometimes found "thistles and thorns where he expected grain."

Water asked, "If I withhold what art thou? dead dry lump." But "If I supply, his [man's] heart and veins rejoice, / If not, soon ends his life, as did his voice." Water was the source of "pearls that dangle at thy Darling's ears." The ocean swallowed up countries and created islands: "Thus Britain fair ('tis thought) was cut from France / Sicily from Italy by the like chance." All of that was nothing compared to the "flood of Noah, / Then wholly perished Earth's ignoble race, / And to this day impairs her beauteous face."

Air was last to speak. Fresh air preserved life, but corrupt air brought "Fevers, Purples, Pox and Pestilence." Air declared, "I am the breath of every living soul." The other elements could not top that.

"Of the Four Humours in Man's Constitution" focused on the four humors of choler, blood, melancholy, and phlegm (discussed in chapter 9), which have to be in balance if someone is to have good health. Anne offered examples of each.

King Henry VI was known for being choleric. Choler said:

Arms, and Arts I claim, and higher things,
The princely qualities befitting Kings,
Whose profound heads I line with policies,
They're held for Oracles, they are so wise, . . .
Their Courage it foe, friend, and Subject awes; . . .
Take Choler from a Prince, what is he more
Than a dead Lion.

The biblical king David was known for blood (fieriness); he was "Judah's most heroic King, / Whose glorious deeds in Arms the world can tell." He was also a musician who "knew well how to handle Sword and Harp" and loved merriment.

Melancholy asked:

What greater Clerk or Politician lives,
Than he whose brain a touch my humour gives? . . .
Reduce the man to his principles, then see
If I have not more part than all you three [the other humors]: . . .
My virtues yours surpass without compare,

The first my constancy that jewel rare:
Choler's too rash this golden gift to hold,
And Sanguine is more fickle manifold, . . .
And what Phlegm is, we know, . . .
Unstable.

Phlegm (calmness) admitted, "Valour I want, no Soldier am 'tis true, . . . / I love no thundering guns, nor bloody wars." Phlegm's excellence was found in the brain and the senses.

Put all of the humors together in "perfect Amity," and there was a "compact body, whole entire."

Anne's playful and serious sides are evident in the lines of "The Four Ages of Man" as she takes readers through "Childhood and Youth, the Manly & Old Age."

Childhood, wearing white and green, was

conceived in sin and born with sorrow,
A nothing, here today and gone tomorrow. . . .
When infancy was past, my childishness
Did act all folly that it could express,
My silliness did only take delight
In that which riper age did scorn and slight.

She included a list of ailments affecting the child as well as his sins: "a perverse will, a love to what's forbid."

Youth had on a crimson suit accented by a green scarf:

With nurture trained up in virtue's schools
Of science, arts and tongues I know the rules,

The manners of the court I also know,
And so likewise what they in the Country do. . . .
Whole nights with Ruffians, Roarers, Fiddlers spend,
To all obscenity mine ears I lend:
All Counsel hate, which tends to make me wise.

He was striving to be a new Adonis.

Middle Age had a sword by his side, and he admitted:

When my wild oats were sown and ripe and mown
I then received an harvest of mine own. . . .
Then with both hands I grasped the world together
Thus out of one extreme into another. . . .
Be my condition mean, I then take pains
My Family to keep, but not for gains.
A Father I, for children must provide;
But if none, then for kindred near allied.
If rich, I'm urged then to gather more,
To bear a post in the world, and feed the poor.
If noble, then mine honour to maintain,
If not, riches nobility can gain. . . .
Yea, justice have I done, was I in place.
To cheer the good, and wicked to deface. . . .
I glory in my wealth I have within.

Old Age was leaning on a staff:

Babe's innocence, youth's wildness I have seen,
And in perplexed middle Age have been:

Sickness, dangers, and anxieties have past,
And on this stage am come to at my last. . . .
In this short pilgrimage I oft have had . . .
Sometimes the Heavens with plenty smiled on me
Sometimes again rained all Adversity.
Sometimes in honour, sometimes in disgrace . . .
Such private changes oft mine eyes have seen.

Old Age had witnessed political changes—"I've seen a Kingdome flourish like a tree, / When it was ruled by that Celestial she [Queen Elizabeth I]"—and wars and the "bloody Popish, hellish miscreants" (meaning Catholics) killing thousands of Irishmen in the insurrection of 1641. At the end of his life he said, "My grinders now are few, my sight doth fail." He was awaiting the "strong Redeemer coming in the Skies" in triumph.

"The Four Seasons of the Year" lets us hear and visualize the countrysides of England and New England. Nightingales are not found in America, but chirping birds and jumping lambs are found in both landscapes. Anne wrote so well that she has readers sweating in the summer sun and shivering in the winter cold.

Spring was all about new life and frogs croaking, nightingales and thrushes chirping, and lambs playing near their mothers. Gardeners were busy planting, and plowmen were toiling in the fields. Fruit trees, grass, honeysuckle, primroses, roses, and double pinks were bursting forth. "The clean housewife" was putting up things to prepare for winter. Anne could not resist this comparison: "Each Season hath his fruit, so hath each Clime:

/ Each man his own peculiar excellence, / But none in all that hath preeminence."

Summer was "wiping the sweat from her face that ran, / With hair all wet the puffing thus began." The sun's "progress to the North now's fully done, / Then retrograde must be my burning Sun." The "parching heat" of the sun was "like as an Oven that long time hath been heat." The month of July from "Julius Caesar took its name, / By Romans celebrated to his fame." Mowers were out in the fields with forks and rakes filling carts, and the reapers with their sickles worked on the wheat, but the "Barley, Rye and Pease should first had place, / Although their bread have not so white a face." The man driving the cart filled with grain was whistling all the way home because his hard work paid off.

The beginning of autumn, September, made Anne think of Adam:

> Sure at this time, time first of all began,
> And in this month was made apostate Man:
> For then in Eden was not only seen,
> Boughs full of leaves, or fruits unripe or green . . .
> Our Grand-Sire as of Paradise made King.

She wrote of "the Northern pole [that] beholdeth not one ray [of the sun]," and autumn required warm clothes, substantial food, such as beef and pork, and "good fire."

In January "Toes and Ears, and Fingers often freeze." With the end of winter (February) "thus the year in Circle runneth round; / Where first it did begin, in the end it's found."

Anne ended the group of poems with this, obviously intended for her father since she signed it "Your dutifull Daughter. A. B.":

> My Subjects bare, my Brain is bad,
> Or better Lines you should have had:
> The first fell in so naturally,
> I knew not how to pass it by;
> The last, though bad I could not mend,
> Accept therefore of what is penned,
> And all the faults that you shall spy
> Shall at your feet for pardon cry.

In the "Four Monarchies," Anne marched through ancient history, rhyming all the way. It was her longest poem in *The Tenth Muse*. She relied heavily on Sir Walter Raleigh's *The History of the World* (1614) because she brought in many battles and soldiers and their leaders, and she named the rulers and their accomplishments. The four monarchies and some of their rulers include (1) Assyrian, beginning with Nimrod through the Persian Cyrus's defeat of the Assyrians; (2) Persian, from Cyrus through Xerxes and beyond; (3) Grecian, focusing on Alexander the Great; and (4) Roman, with its founder, Romulus.

She dated the Assyrian "beginning under Nimrod, 131 Years after the Flood." One of his heirs built up Nineveh, whose walls were "so broad three Chariots run abrest there might." She included a female ruler, too, after the death of Ninus: "His wife Semiramis usurped the Throne; / She like a brave Virago played the Rex / And was both shame and glory of her Sex." Many aspersions were cast on Semiramis's character, perhaps by the Greeks, suggested Anne:

> But were her virtues more or less, or none,
> She for her potency must go alone.
> Her wealth she shewed in building Babylon,
> Admired of all, but equalized of none.

Then Nebuchadnezzar had "wise Daniel and his fellowes" among his captives:

> His Image Judah's Captives worship not,
> Although the Furnace be seven times more hot.
> His dreams wise Daniel doth expound full well,
> And his unhappy change with grief foretell.

The Persians under Cyrus defeated the Assyrians. Anne brought up Artaxerxes and Esther ("how her Country-men from spoil she freed"), Ezra, and Nehemiah (who went to Jerusalem, "his city dear," to rebuild its walls). The last king was Darius:

> Whose Wars, and losses we may better tell,
> In Alexander's reign who did him quell,
> How from the top of world's felicity,
> He fell to depth of greatest misery.

The Grecian monarchy began with Alexander the Great:

> Great were the Gifts of nature which he had,
> His education much to those did add:
> By art and nature both he was made fit,
> To 'complish that which long before was writ.

Alexander's conquests were many, and Anne touched on all of them, right down to numbers of combatants ("forty five thousand Alexander had" in one battle) and tactics. She briefly touched on Cleopatra and Mark Antony in Egypt.

The last monarchy was Rome: "From small beginnings did it grow, / To fill the world with terror and with woe." Anne warned the reader that the section about Rome because of "shortness of time and inability" forced her "to a confused brevity." Yet "in this Chaos, one shall easily spy / The vast Limbs of a mighty Monarchy." This was the shortest poem of the four, and it began with the founder of Rome and its first king, Romulus. She explained how he built the city, formed a government, and chose senators. She mentioned a few others but ended the poem abruptly with Tarquin as the last king of the Romans: "The Government they change, a new one bring / And people swear never to accept of King."

A change of pace from the long poems was a poem for her father, which was straight from the heart and less from the head:

> Most truly honoured, and as truly dear,
> If worth in me, or ought I do appear,
> Who can of right better demand the same?
> Then may your worthy self from whom it came.

The principle might yield a greater sum,
Yet handled ill, amounts but to this crumb;
My stock's so small, I know not how to pay,
My Bond remains in force unto this day;
Yet for part payment take this simple mite,
Where nothing's to be had Kings lose their right
Such is my debt, I may not say forgive,
But as I can, I'll pay it while I live:
Such is my bond, none can discharge but I,
Yet paying is not paid until I die.

Guillame de Salluste Du Bartas, a French poet, was a favorite of Anne's, and in 1641, she composed "In honour of Du Bartas." He dazzled her:

Among the happy wits this age hath shown,
Great, dear, sweet Bartas thou art matchless known. . . .
My dazzled sight of late reviewed thy lines,
Where Art, and more than Art, in nature shines. . . .
Thus weak brained I, reading thy lofty style,
Thy profound learning . . . ;
Thy Art in natural Philosophy,
Thy Saintlike mind in grave Divinity;
Thy piercing skill in high Astronomy.

He also was gifted in anatomy, music, and state policy, and valorous in war. She was convinced that "Bartas fame shall last while starrs do stand, / And whilst there's Air or Fire, or Sea or Land." Alas, she proved to be wrong on that point; the popularity of his work waned by the late seventeenth century, and most of us in the twenty-first century are unfamiliar with Bartas.

Two other short poems are notable because they are so different from the long ones. The first is "David's Lamentation for Saul and Jonathan," based on 2 Samuel 1:19 when David mourned the deaths of both men: "valiant Saul" and "lovely Jonathan" who fell in battle. The second is "The Vanity of All Worldly Things," which begins, "As he said vanity, so vain say I, / Oh! vanity, O vain all under Sky." Whether wealth or beauty, youth or "manly age," all is vanity—except

> that living Crystal Fount,
> Who drinks thereof, the world doth naught account. . . .
> This pearl of price, this tree of life, this spring
> Who is possessed of, shall reign a King.
> Nor change of state, nor cares shall ever see,
> But wear his crown unto eternity.

We do not know how many copies of Anne's books sold in England or New England, but some historians believe that most Puritan homes in New England had a copy.[10] We do know that a bookseller catalog for William London noted in 1658 that hers was one of "the most vendible books in England."[11]

Finding women writers who were contemporaries of Anne Bradstreet in either New England or England poses a challenge. Most were in England, and most did not have the settled home life that Anne enjoyed. Many more women than scholars have identified might have been writing, but their work did not survive or was not published.

In New England, one woman writer lost "her understanding and reason, which had been growing upon her divers years," according to John Winthrop. That woman was Anne Hopkins, the wife of Governor Edward Hopkins of Connecticut. In 1645, Anne Hopkins was taken to Boston for treatment, but she was beyond help. Her husband left her there with her brother, David Yale. Winthrop explained further about why she was in that sad condition: she gave herself "wholly to reading and writing, and had written many books. . . . For if she had attended her household affairs, and such things as belong to women, and not gone out of her way . . . to meddle in such things as are proper for men, whose minds are stronger, etc., she had kept her wits and might have improved them usefully and honorably in the place God had set her." Nothing survives of what she wrote.[12]

A family member of Anne Bradstreet's brother-in-law John Woodbridge was condemned for her *Scripture-Prophecies Opened, Which are to be accomplished in these last times, which do attend the second coming of Christ* published in England. The author was Elizabeth Avery, a sister of Thomas Parker and an aunt of John Woodbridge who regarded herself as a "visionary prophet." John had come to New England with his uncle Thomas Parker, who was an assistant of Nathaniel Ward in Ipswich, and they were early settlers of Newbury, Massachusetts. Elizabeth Avery remained in Newbury, England. After she lost three children, Avery felt that life had lost all meaning: "[I was left] in a horror, as if I were in hell, none could comfort me, nothing could satisfy me, no friends, nothing."[13] Then she experienced her enlightenment, and she had to write about it. Unlike the family's approval of Anne's works, which were in keeping with church discipline and proper decorum, they responded harshly to Elizabeth's book. Her brother Thomas published *The Copy of a Letter Written by Mr. Thomas Parker, Pastor of the Church of Newbury in New-England, to His Sister, Mrs. Elizabeth Avery, Sometimes of Newbury in the County of Berks, Touching Sundry Opinions by Her Professed and Maintained* in London in 1650 (the same year that Anne's *Tenth Muse* was published) and denounced Elizabeth in no uncertain terms. One unforgettable line from Thomas was this: "Your printing of a Book, beyond the custom of your Sex, doth rankly smell." And his nephew Benjamin Woodbridge, who composed a poem praising Anne, wrote the introduction to his uncle's *Letter*.[14]

Also in England, Lady Mary Wroth (1587–1653), who was a niece of Sir Philip Sidney, wrote fiction and poetry. She was another young woman whose father, Sir Robert Sidney, took a great interest in her education. She was the first Englishwoman to publish an original work of fiction, *Urania* (1621), and the book also contained her sonnet sequence, *Pamphilia to Amphilanthus*. The book became controversial because many of the "fictional" characters were people she knew that were recognizable to readers, and the "characters" were much displeased with their portrayals. She was in debt most of her life following the death of her husband, and she was involved in a scandalous relationship with her first cousin.[15]

Englishwoman Aphra Behn (1640–89) wrote and published numerous plays, a novel, and poetry, and she managed to support herself by writing. That was *after* she was widowed and became a spy for King Charles II during the war with the Netherlands. She is buried in Westminster Abbey, a true national honor.[16]

Anne Killigrew (1660–85) was the daughter of a doctor in London, and she spent her life in the court of the Restoration. Her father published her book, *Poems by Mrs. Anne Killegrew*, following her death from smallpox. Poet John Dryden was eloquent in praising her poetic talent. She also had artistic talent and painted portraits of the king's family members. Since she died so young, one has to wonder how much more she could have accomplished if she had lived past her twenty-five years.[17]

Like of all these women, Anne Bradstreet felt compelled to write, but unlike some of them, she was fortunate to be published and praised. Cotton Mather, minister of North Church in Boston, Massachusetts, and grandson of John Cotton and Richard Mather, was born near the end of Anne's life. He wrote the classic church history of New England, *Magnalia Christi Americana*, and he included Anne as one of the very few women in the seven volumes. He observed that she was celebrated in both Englands for her poetic works, and he stated that her poems, "diverse times Printed, have afforded a grateful entertainment . . . and a monument for her memory beyond the stateliest marbles."[18]

LAMENTATIONS

A lengthy season of lamentations beginning in 1648 beset Anne and the colony. An unwanted invitation to make a new home in Ireland, the death of her beloved father, and recurring sicknesses and weaknesses weighed heavily on Anne. The trials and executions of two women, one an accused witch and one a Quaker, left indelible blots on the Massachusetts Bay Colony.

Hearing the words *witchcraft* and *New England*, most people think of the Salem witchcraft trials in the latter part of the seventeenth century. But years earlier, in June 1648, a midwife of Charlestown named Margaret Jones was indicted for witchcraft and placed on trial in Boston. From 1645 to 1648 in England, more than one hundred people were convicted of witchcraft and sentenced to death, most by hanging. Historians refer to what had been happening in England as a witch hunt. Hearing about these numbers made the people of Massachusetts increasingly wary: If so many witches were in England, could New England have some too? The General Court thought that there was at least Margaret Jones.

Governor Winthrop oversaw the proceedings of the trial, and Deputy Governor Dudley and assistants Simon Bradstreet, John Winthrop Jr., and a few others also participated. The Laws and Liberties of Massachusetts identified witchcraft as a capital crime, citing Leviticus 20:27. The court found Jones guilty and sentenced her to be hanged in Boston Common. Jones's was the first execution of a witch in Massachusetts, but it was not the first (or the last) in New England.[1]

John Winthrop died in March 1649, having completed a three-year term as governor in 1648. John Endicott immediately followed him as governor. For ten years after Winthrop's death, the colony enjoyed more prosperity than it ever had. Simon Bradstreet continued to prosper, and he became a partner with two other men in owning a ship. Both men had been among the early settlers of Ipswich. George Carr was a shipwright, and Richard Saltonstall was the son of Sir Richard Saltonstall and had come over on the *Arbella*. The captain of their vessel was Elias Parkman, and he went up and down the coast from Massachusetts to Connecticut carrying cargo. The business relationship proved to be stormy sailing, however, because the captain owed all three men money and they had to take him to court. They knew that he had made five or six trips but refused to pay what he owed them, and they also knew he had the money to pay.[2]

Thomas Dudley served his last term as governor in 1650. John Endicott was chosen governor again in 1651, and Dudley, the last time as deputy governor. They had to deal with an unusual and much unwanted proposal from Oliver Cromwell that required all of their combined diplomatic skills. Cromwell suggested strongly that some or all of the people in Massachusetts should move to Ireland. Since Cromwell and the English army had decimated the population of Ireland, there was a need for strong Puritans to keep popery from getting the upper hand there.

Daniel Denison and some New England ministers wrote a letter thanking Cromwell for the honor of his proposal but reminded him that the Lord had called them to New England; if the Lord called them to Ireland, they would cheerfully go. None of them did. Endicott and Dudley replied nicely to Cromwell and then to the Lord General, praising his efforts in England and Ireland. They offered several reasons why the colonists were not going to leave for Ireland: from enjoying "the liberties of the gospel" to having plentiful food and good health in New England, to working at converting the Native Americans and not being engaged in war. They would not stop anyone who chose to go, however.[3] So was another crisis in the colony averted, and Anne and her family did not have to pack for an ocean voyage to Ireland and try to establish a home in another kind of wilderness. Cromwell soon had too much to handle in England to pursue the idea further.

Four years after the death of John Winthrop, the man with whom he had worked to create a city upon a hill, Thomas Dudley, died. In his later years, he had become harder and tougher with those who did not share his views about religion, and he began to question the tolerance of his son-in-law Simon Bradstreet. His daughter Anne remained steadfast in the love and support of her father, no matter how tough he was with others, and wrote, "To the Memory of my dear and ever honoured Father Thomas Dudley Esq; Who deceased, July 31, 1653, and of his Age, 77."

She presented her "Lamentations" for her "Father, Guide, Instructor too, /To whom I ought whatever I could do." She listed his merits: a founder of New England who "spent his state, his strength, and years with care / That After-comers in them might share. / True Patriot of this little Commonweal." He was "Truth's friend" who loved "true Religion." She continued,

> My Father's God, be God of me and mine.
> Upon the earth he did not build his nest,
> But as a Pilgrim, what he had, possessed. . . .
> Those titles loathed, which some too much do love
> For truly his ambition lay above. . . .
> His thoughts were more sublime, his actions wise.

After years of toil, he was now resting in heaven:

> His pious Footsteps followed by his race,
> At last will bring us to that happy place
> Where we with joy each other's face shall see,
> And parted more by death shall never be.[4]

Dudley had spent twenty-three years of his life managing the affairs of the Massachusetts Bay Colony and was "never put under any investigation of his administrations, civil, military or judicial."[5]

Thomas Dudley was a poet too, it seems, and these lines were found in his pocket after his death:

Let men of God in Courts and Churches watch,

Over such as do a Toleration hatch,

Lest that ill Egg bring forth a Cockatrice

To poison all with Heresy and Vice.

If Men be left and otherwise Combine,

My epitaph's I died no Libertine.[6]

Dudley left behind an estate of 356 acres in Roxbury alone. He was buried in that town in a tomb covered with white marble, and the inscription plate on it was made of pewter. The story goes that when Boston was under siege during the Revolutionary War, soldiers removed the plate and melted it down for bullets.[7]

Anne took comfort in knowing that her father lived to see the births of all of her children. Anne and Simon had had two more sons, Dudley in 1648 and John in 1652. John was born two years after the publication of *The Tenth Muse*, when his mother was forty years old, and two years after Anne's half-brother Paul was born. And Thomas Dudley knew that Anne's oldest child, Samuel, graduated from Harvard College in 1653.

The lives of Anne and Simon and their children proceeded smoothly with nothing remarkable until their daughter Dorothy married Seaborn Cotton, a Harvard graduate and the son of John Cotton, in the summer of 1654. As a magistrate, Dorothy's father, Simon, performed the ceremony. Seaborn had been so smitten with the nineteen-year-old that he rode from Boston, where he lived, to Andover to see her whenever he could. The young couple moved to Connecticut and then to Hampton, New Hampshire, where Seaborn served as a minister. Anne's children were starting to leave the nest, as their mother knew they would.

That did not mean she was happy about it, especially since they did not remain nearby.

Whether Anne's health, never vigorous in the first place, started a slow decline soon after her father's death or the problems began precipitously, she had almost a year of debilitating illness beginning in the summer of 1656. Her youngest child was just four.

She had a fainting fit that lasted two or three days, and Simon was gone when it happened. That made it worse because Simon was her "chiefest comforter on Earth." She wrote in the manuscript that she left for her children, "Lord, why should I doubt any more when thou hast given me such assured Pledges of thy Love?" She knew that he was her Creator, that Christ was her Brother. But apparently doubts about her faith continued, even though she wrote that God manifested his love to her. She fervently hoped that she would be "no more afraid of Death, but even desire to be dissolved," and be with the Lord, "best of All." She added, "O Lord, let me never forget thy Goodness, nor question thy faithfulness to me, for thou art my God. . . . O, never let Satan prevail against me, but strengthen my faith in Thee, 'till I shall attain the end of my hopes, even the Salvation of my Soul. Come, Lord Jesus; come quickly."[8] This last line became a recurring refrain from her until her last days.

A month later, she wrote, "After much weakness and sickness when my spirits were worn out, and many times my faith weak likewise, the Lord was pleased to uphold my drooping heart, and to manifest his Love to me. . . . God doth not afflict willingly, nor take delight in grieving the children of men; he hath no benefit by my adversity, nor is he the better for my prosperity." He did all for her advantage so that she might gain something from it:

> And if he knows that weakness and a frail body is the best to make me a vessel fit for his use, why should I not bear it, not only willingly but joyfully? The Lord knows I dare not desire that health that sometimes I have had lest my heart should be drawn from him, and set upon the world.
>
> Now I can wait, looking every day when my Saviour shall call for me. Lord grant that while I live I may do that service I am able in this frail Body, and be in continual expectation of my change. . . . O let me ever see Thee that Art invisible, and I shall not be unwilling to come, though by so rough a Messenger.[9]

The spring of the next year, Anne was sick almost the entire time until May 11: "I had a sore sickness, and weakness took hold of me." She had a few respites when she could fulfill some, but not all, of her duties to God and family. She said, "That which I now chiefly labour for is a contented, thankful heart under my affliction and weakness, being it is the will of God."[10]

She wrote this untitled poem just after the note about her illness:

> My Sun's returned with healing wings,
> My Soul and Body doth rejoice:
> My heart exalts, and praises sings
> To him that heard my wailing Voice.

> My winter's past, my storms are gone,
> And former clouds seem now all fled;
> But, if they must eclipse again,
> I'll run where I was succored.

Her shelter from the storm was God, "so wondrous great."[11]

Despite her hopes and prayers for strength, she had to write in late September, "It pleased God to visit me with my old Distemper of weakness and fainting, but not in that fore manner sometimes he hath." She wanted to submit to him willingly and thankfully; she trusted that he brought that upon her because of his abundant love for her "straying Soul which in prosperity is too much in love with the world. I have found by experience I can no more live without correction than without food."

She wrote to her children, "Thus have ye seen the many sicknesses and weaknesses that I have passed through; to the end that, if you meet with the like, you may have recourse to the same God who hath heard and delivered me." He could do the same for them, and they should thank him and walk more closely with him.[12]

Within two months, Anne had occasion to write a poem about her son Samuel. He published *An Almanack for the Year of Our Lord 1657* in Cambridge as a tutor of the college, and it included a poem he wrote about the god Apollo. But life as a scholar and poet did not suit him. He sailed for England on November 6 so that he could be trained in medicine.[13] Anne's poem was really more like a prayer asking God to keep him safe and to bring her son back to her. Samuel was the "Son of Prayers, of vows, of tears. / The child I stayed for many years."

Years ago, God had heard her prayer for a child and had given Samuel to her: "He's mine, but more, O Lord, thine own, / For sure thy Grace on him is shown."[14]

Composing that poem about one child must have sparked the idea of writing one about all of her children. By June of 1658, she was ready with comments about her "eight birds hatched in one nest, / Four Cocks there were, and Hens the rest." She did her best to rear them with "pain and care, / Nor cost, nor labour did I spare, / Till at the last they felt their wing."

Samuel, the "Chief of the Brood," flew to far-off regions, and she sent her "mournful chirps" after him until he returned or she passed away.

The second bird took flight and left with her mate. A "prettier bird no where was seen" than Dorothy.

The third had also left with a mate "loving and true," and Anne "placed no small delight" on her. Sarah married Richard Hubbard of Ipswich in 1658; her father performed the ceremony, as he had done for Dorothy. Born in England, Richard graduated from Harvard College the same year as Sarah's brother Samuel, and Richard became a wealthy landowner.

The next boy, Simon, went to Harvard "to chat among that learned crew."

The other three remained at home in the "nest, / Until they're grown" and take flight like the others.

Like most mothers, Anne tried to keep them from harm and wanted the best for them:

O to your safety have an eye,
So happy may you live and die: . . .

My age I will not once lament,
But sing, my time so near is spent.
And from the top bough take my flight,
Into a country beyond sight, . . .
When each of you shall in your nest
Among your young ones take your rest,
In chirping language, oft them tell,
You had a Dam that loved you well, . . .
She showed you joy and misery;
Taught what was good, and what was ill . . .
Farewell, my birds, farewell, adieu,
I happy am, if well with you.[15]

While Anne had her eyes on domestic and health concerns, Simon and the courts had to rule on intrusion into the colony by Anabaptists and Quakers. The General Court ordered the banishment of Anabaptists in 1644 and in 1658 ordered the same for Quakers.[16] To the court, Quakers were heretics. The law read, in part, "There is a cursed sect of heretics lately risen in the world, . . . Quakers, who take upon them to be immediately sent of God, and infallibly assisted by the spirit to speak and write blasphemous opinions, despising government and the order of God in church and commonwealth, speaking evil of dignities, reproaching and reviling magistrates and ministers" in order to turn the people from the truth faith and to their "pernicious ways."[17] The law also named the punishments for Quakers who violated it by teaching their ways, speaking out in opposition to the court, or importing, circulating, or concealing Quaker books. Shipmasters were not to bring them to New England.

Violators could be fined, imprisoned, or whipped, or they could have their ears cropped. If they repeated their crime, they could be imprisoned and then banished from the town. If they came back again after the banishment, the penalty was death. All of these punishments were meted out.

Quakers and later Quaker historians had nothing good to say about the Puritans in charge of these proceedings, and Simon Bradstreet came in for his share of criticism as persecuting prosecutor. Serving as magistrate in the Ipswich court, Bradstreet was "a man hardened in Blood and a cruel persecutor,"[18] according to Quaker historian George Bishop in his book about the sufferings of the Quakers from 1656 to 1660 in New England. Bradstreet's brother-in-law Daniel Denison was in charge of the physical punishment at Ipswich, and he too earned a place in the Quaker history books as a persecutor.[19]

One woman was not the only Quaker to be executed in the colony, but she was a memorable example. Mary Dyer, a Puritan, had been a follower of Anne Hutchinson and had left Boston after Anne was banished. Dyer and her husband went to Rhode Island with the Hutchinsons. Dyer then went back to England, where she became a Quaker and returned to Massachusetts to present her faith there, although the ban on Quakers was in place. The court, presided over by Governor John Endicott, ordered her to leave the colony, but she refused to obey. She was stripped to the waist and whipped, convicted of blasphemy, and thrown out of the colony. She came back again and was condemned to death for sedition and returning after her banishment. She was hanged on Boston Common in 1660.[20]

The English government took notice of the colony's

mistreatment of Quakers in addition to other complaints brought against it, and the well-being of the colony in general and Simon Bradstreet in particular was threatened as a result. Almost simultaneously with the restoration of the monarchy in Old England and the king's attempts to bring his people back together—and to rule without the influence of Puritanism—a weary Anne started slipping away from New England.

"WEARY PILGRIM, NOW AT REST"

I n 1660, Charles II was restored to the throne of England, and that ended the Puritans' rule of the country led by the two Cromwells. Historian John Richard Green stated that with the Restoration "the whole face of England was changed in an instant. All that was noblest and best in Puritanism was whirled away with its pettiness and its tyranny in the current of the nation's hate. Religion had been turned into a system of political and social oppression, and it fell with that system's fall."[1] Determining what to do about uniting the fragmented church in his country was only one of the king's major problems. The governmental coffers were not adequately filled, Catholic France was flexing its strong muscles, and there were still within his country people who had opposed him and his father. His Parliament had many strong Anglican members who enabled the Anglican Church to reassert itself and regain strength.

Samuel Bradstreet, studying medicine in England and

witnessing the governmental changes, must have wondered about possible repercussions in Massachusetts. When he returned in 1661 and started his practice in Boston, he did not have to wait long to find out. But first he heard of the recent medical news from the family.

His mother had been free of serious illness for four years, which made the physical blow she received from January to May 1661 all the harder to bear. During that period, she was "by fits very ill and weak." She had a fever in early May that lasted four days, and the hot weather made it even more tedious. But, Anne said, "it pleased the Lord to support my heart in his goodness, and to hear my Prayers, and to deliver me out of adversity." Her thankful poem also touched on her doubts:

> Lord, whilst my fleeting time shall last,
> Thy Goodness let me Tell.
> And new Experience I have gained,
> My future Doubts repel.[2]

She had barely recovered and was still weak when Simon suffered a "burning Ague" in June. At the thought of losing him, she was beset with fears and sorrows, and her "heart did faint." The Lord restored Simon to health, and Anne praised him who did not leave her "Soul as destitute; / Nor turned his ear away from me."[3]

Her fervent prayers did not cease for an ill family member (her prayers were unceasing for the family anyway) because their daughter Hannah also had a dangerous fever from which she recovered. Yet she had been close to death. "When death did seem even to approach, / And life was ended near," Anne asked God, "Let her Conversation say, / She loves thee all thy Days." Hannah had married Andrew Wiggin of Exeter, New Hampshire, the son of the governor of that colony, two years earlier.[4]

Then her son Samuel returned in July, much to Anne's relief. She had not seen him for four years. Her poem was full of excitement, but it also revealed the thoughts she had been harboring about his safety. Her fears turned to joy, her sighs to song, and her tears to smiles. She praised God for keeping Simon safe from pirates and the sinking of ships and for helping him survive smallpox, which had raced through England in 1660 and killed even members of the royal family. God had also provided friends for Samuel everywhere. She added:

> On Eagle's wings him hither brought [See Ex. 19:4.]
> Through Want and Dangers manifold;
> And thou hath granted my Request,
> That I thy Mercies might behold.[5]

Anne soon had to shift her prayerful requests for God's protection of a loved one in England when her husband carried out another duty for the colony. The colonists of Massachusetts were uncertain what to expect from King Charles II, who was born the year that the *Arbella* delivered her passengers to the shores of New England. Rather than wait for him to make the first move, they took a proactive approach and appointed a committee to develop a state paper to deliver to him. Simon Bradstreet drew up the document that was adopted by the General Court in June 1661, which set forth the rights and liberties of the colony under the charter, followed by a declaration of allegiance, loyalty, and duty to the king.

In due course, Charles II's government demanded a response from Massachusetts about the persecution of Quakers and other complaints lodged against the colony.[6] The representatives who took the colonists' case to England were Simon Bradstreet, Rev. John Norton, and John Hull, the silversmith and head of the colony's mint. They were supposed to sail in the middle of January, but Rev. Norton was ill and had to recover, so they did not leave until February 10, 1662. It took them until early April to reach London.

Immediately Anne started writing poems about her beloved Simon and asked the Lord to keep safe her "dear friend." He had gone on this mission at the Lord's command, "Nor naught could keep him back; / Then let thy promise joy his heart: / O help, and be not slack." She confessed how weak and frail she was and implored God not to turn his face from her. She asked for Simon to have success in his mission and said,

> Remember, Lord, thy folk whom thou
> To wilderness hath brought. . . .
> Lord, let my eyes see once Again
> Him whom thou gavest me.[7]

In another poem about her solitary hours in Simon's absence, she spoke of her "daily moans" and "dropping tears." She had both longings and fears, but as in former times she looked to God to "uphold [her] fainting Soul!" She ended by saying, "Unless thou help, what can I do / But still my frailty show?"[8]

Anne had more reason to fear for Simon's safety in England than perhaps she realized. There was the real possibility that he and Norton could have been prosecuted by relatives of the Quakers who had been executed in Massachusetts. Letters arrived in New England saying that both had been detained, but that did not prove to be true. Receiving letters from Simon brought some relief to Anne's "fainting heart" even as she asked God to return her husband to her. Each poem was so full of references to tears, doubts, and fears that Anne must have been on pins and needles all those months until Simon arrived safely in New England on September 3. Upon his return, she thanked God for his great mercies, "In number numberless / Impossible for to recount / Or any way express."[9]

The men had gone to Charles's court and delivered their letters to the Lord Chancellor. Hull wrote in his diary that after several comings and goings to the court, he and the other two men "had fair promises of a full grant" of their "whole desire in the country's behalf" from the king. Then "sundry things" were ordered that "seemed somewhat inconsistent with our patent [charter] and former privileges," especially in regard to "good laws and customs." Those "sundry things" came under serious review by the General Court, and they took measures to hide and protect the colony's charter—just in case the king had any ideas about coming for it.[10]

The king did keep his eye on the New England colonies, but the issues at home and in Europe preoccupied him. Then two disasters hit his capital of London. In the spring and exceedingly hot summer of 1665, he and his court had to flee when the Black Death took the lives of more than one hundred thousand people in the city. Then in early September 1666, the Great Fire burned more than 80 percent of London, including houses, churches, and businesses. The king did not flee that time but stayed to oversee firefighting measures in hopes of saving the city. Despite his and his men's best efforts, the fire was just too overwhelming to contain. If there was any good news to be told, it was that most human residents survived the conflagration, but the rats and their plague-carrying fleas did not.

Anne and Simon had their own great fire that devastated their home in the summer of 1666. Anne had a fear of fire that dated back more than thirty years to an incident at the home of her parents and siblings in Newtowne. In that fire, the hearth of the hall chimney burned all night on a principal beam of the house, and it was not discovered until the next morning. The flames had burned out before reaching gunpowder stored nearby. More recently, in 1665, the home in Ipswich belonging to her sister Patience burned. A female servant suspected of setting it was taken to court, but she was acquitted, and the cause was ruled unknown.

The Bradstreets' house in Andover was made of heavy timbers, and it had a huge chimney in the center. The fire destroyed furniture that had arrived from Lincolnshire, family portraits, a library of about eight hundred books, clothing and household items, and Anne's papers.[11]

Anne's "Verses on the Burning of the House, July 10, 1666" conveyed her terror and her chagrin at what occurred on that fateful day. She and the family awakened during the night to "Piteous shrieks of dreadful voice. / That fearful sound of fire and fire." Everyone safely fled the burning house, and she watched the "flame consume my dwelling place." But at some point she "could no longer look," so she blessed "the Name that gave and took, / That laid my goods now in the dust."

Days later, as she walked past the ruins of that home, "My sorrowing eye aside did cast, / And here and there the places spy / Where oft I sat, and long did lie." She recalled the trunk and the chest that were then in ashes. She missed the meals and the guests that she had known under that roof. She bid adieu to all of it: "Farewell my Pelf, farewell my Store. / The world no longer let me Love, / My hope and Treasure lies Above."[12]

For some time, Anne had been revising her *Tenth Muse*, and she lost all of the revisions in the fire. We do have "The Author to Her Book" that summed up her comments on the first edition: "Thou ill-formed offspring of my feeble brain, / Who after birth didst by my side remain, / Till snatched from thence by friends, less wise then true," who took the book abroad to be "exposed to public view." (These comments added to the discussion about whether the manuscript was taken to England without her knowledge.) She explained why she was working on the revisions: "Thy visage was so irksome in my sight; / Yet being mine own, at length affection would / Thy blemishes amend, if so I could."[13]

In addition to the revisions, "An Apology" from Anne, which appeared in the second edition of her book, indicated her efforts to finish the Roman section of "The Four Monarchies":

> To finish what's begun, was my intent,
> My thoughts and my endeavours thereto bent;

> Essays I many made but still gave out . . .
>
> At length resolved, when many years had past,
>
> To prosecute my story to the last;
>
> And . . . I hours not few did spend,
>
> And weary lines . . . I many penned.

But her "papers fell a prey to the raging fire. / And thus my pains (with better things) I lost, / Which none had cause to wail, nor I to boast." She was unwilling to attempt to do more since "I have suffered wrack."[14]

The new house, built like the first, was completed in 1667 and furnished with new things. Yet Anne probably did not enjoy it. She suffered physically and emotionally in this second house in Andover for the remaining years of her life.

Samuel Bradstreet married Mercy Tyng in 1662, not long after he returned from his medical training in England. They had very few years of happiness before multiple tragedies hit them, and one early blessing was the birth of their first child, Elizabeth. She died when she was one and a half in August 1665, and Anne mourned her passing as she bade farewell to the "sweet babe, the pleasure of mine eye." She had to take comfort in knowing that the blest babe was "settled in an Everlasting state." Next her namesake, Anne, died of a fever when she was three and a half in June 1669: "With troubled heart & trembling hand I write, / The Heavens have changed to sorrow my delight. / But yet a while, and I shall go to thee." She knew the child was "as a withering flower, / That's here today, perhaps gone in an hour."[15] Next Simon's namesake died at one month old in November 1669:

No sooner come, but gone, . . .
Acquaintance short, yet parting caused us weep,
Three flowers, two scarcely blown, the last in the bud,
Cropped by the Almighty's hand; yet he is good.

Before another year had passed, in September 1670, Anne lost her daughter-in-law and another grandchild while Samuel was sailing to Jamaica. He left his daughter Mercy in Anne and Simon's care. Samuel's wife, Mercy, was only twenty-eight, and she spent a week after childbirth "in pain and woe, / And then her sorrows all at once did go." The baby, another Anne, died before her. The poem in Mercy's memory was as much to comfort Samuel as to express Anne's sorrow. He had "lost both Tree and fruit," and Anne's "bruised heart" lay "sobbing at the Root." She knew that Mercy loved Samuel "more (it seemed) than her own life." The child Mercy, born in 1667, remained with her Bradstreet grandparents as long as Anne lived, and Simon Bradstreet's will noted that he educated and maintained her.

Anne and Simon's daughter Mercy was still at home, and she helped her parents care for her niece Mercy. Before long, however, she had to oversee her mother's care with the assistance of servants. Anne experienced more fevers and fainting spells, and her body became frailer and frailer. For the last couple of years of her life, she was almost an invalid.

Consumption took Anne from her loved ones. Some people may believe that consumption and tuberculosis are the same ailment, but they are not. Tuberculosis may lead to consumption. The sufferer begins with tuberculosis, and if it is left untreated (and there was no treatment for it in the seventeenth century), it leads to its final stage, which is consumption. The first attack is mild, and subsequent attacks become more severe. Anne also had a huge ulcer on her arm that did not heal, and it was likely a lesion caused by the tuberculosis. A few months before Anne's death, her daughter Dorothy Cotton passed away. The rest of Anne's children survived her, and her son Simon wrote of her passing that she had "wasted to skin and bone." His "ever-honoured and dear mother was translated to heaven"[16] on September 16, 1672, at the age of sixty.

John Norton, the nephew of Rev. John Norton and a recent graduate of Harvard College, wrote a funeral elegy: "Upon that Pattern and Patron of Virtue, the truly pious, peerless & matchless Gentlewoman, Mrs. Anne Bradstreet, all virtuous, Mirror of her Age, Glory of her Sex." He stated,

> Did not the lowering heavens seem to express
> The world's great loss, and their unhappiness? . . .
> How do the Goddess of verse, the learned choir
> Lament their rival Quill, which all admire? . . .
> Some do for anguish weep, for anger I
> That Ignorance should live, and Art should die.

He praised her, whose "breast was a brave Palace, a Broad-street, / Where all heroic ample thoughts did meet."[17]

The problem is that no one thought to keep a record of her burial place, or it has been lost. Some think she was buried in Roxbury with her father and mother. The North Andover Historical Society believes that her final resting place was in the Old Burying Ground in Andover. We do not know where to place the wreath of thyme or parsley that Anne was willing to accept.

Anne left behind daughter Mercy, who married Nathaniel Wade a few weeks after Anne's death. Son Simon was married to his cousin Lucy Woodbridge and became a minister in New London, Connecticut. John became a gentleman farmer in Topsfield and married Sarah, the daughter of Rev. William Perkins. Dudley Bradstreet became a town clerk and a magistrate in Andover, and he married the widow Ann Wood the year after his mother's death. Daughter Sarah lost her first husband and married Samuel Ward. Hannah and Andrew Wiggin lived in North Hampshire. Son Samuel, the medical doctor, married again but remained in Jamaica and did not return to New England. Anne and Simon eventually had more than forty grandchildren.

What of Anne's beloved husband, Simon? There is no doubt that he felt she was his beloved Anne. Unlike most widowers, he did not remarry immediately. He apparently could not live in the Andover house without his poetess Anne and moved to Salem, leaving the Andover house to their son Dudley. He waited four years after her death, when he was seventy-three, and married Anne Downing Gardner, a widow. He was elected deputy governor and governor of Massachusetts. After more than sixty years of public service, Simon died at age ninety-four, the last survivor of the founders who came from England in 1630. He was buried at Salem.

We do not have to wonder what Anne was thinking at the end of her life or what she really believed because she left a record, thanks to nudging from her son Simon to leave something for him to have of her after she was gone. These writings, which she began in 1664, appeared posthumously in the 1678 edition of her book.

She nudged her son back by writing, "Children do naturally rather follow the failings than the virtues of their predecessors, but I am persuaded better things of you." She wrote seventy-seven "Meditations Divine and Moral" and a commentary about her faith over the years. Of her "Meditations" she said, "Such as they are I bequeath to you: small legacies are accepted by true friends, much more by duty full children."[18] Some are brief, and others are long paragraphs. Just a few are offered here:

2. Many can speak well, but few can do well. We are better scholars in Theory than the practical part, but he is a true Christian that is proficient in both.

7. The finest bread hath the least bran; the purest honey, the least wax; and the sincerest Christian, the least self-love.

16. That house which is not often swept, makes the cleanly inhabitant soon loathe it, and that heart which is not continually purifying itself, is no fit temple for the spirit of God to dwell in.

34. Dim eyes are the concomitants of old age; and short-sightedness, in those that are eyes of a Republic, foretells a declining State.

43. Fire hath its force abated by water, not by wind; and anger must be allayed by cold words, and not by blustering threats.

77. There was never any one man that had all excellences, let his parts, natural and acquired, spiritual and moral, be never so large, yet he stands in need of something which

another man hath . . . which shows us perfection is not below, as also, that God will have us beholden to one another.

In the comments about herself she addressed her "Dear Children" because she feared that when she was on her deathbed, she might not be able to speak to them, especially since they were scattered in the world. She wanted to speak the truth and set forth God's glory, not hers. She told about God's dealing with her from childhood to the time she wrote these words. She said, "As I have brought you into the world, and with great pains, weakness, cares, and fears brought you to this, I now travail in birth again of you till Christ be formed in you."[19]

She strongly believed that, in God's dealings with her, he never allowed her to "sit loose from him" very long. If she did, "one affliction or other" made her evaluate what was amiss. Her heart was not out of order long before she "expected correction for it." The correction took the form of sickness, weakness, pains, physical and spiritual, doubts, and "fears of God's displeasure." Or perhaps one of her children was sick, or she was "chastened by losses in estate." Yet in such times the Lord "manifested the most Love" to her. She followed the example of King David in asking the Lord to search her and try her and lead her in the everlasting way (Psalm 139:23). When she did all that, she found a sin that God wanted to reform or some neglected duty that he wanted her to do. With God's help, she endeavored to perform "his righteous commands."

She compared herself to a wayward child who had just felt the rod on her back or had seen the rod about to be applied but who almost immediately forgot God and herself. She wrote, "Before I was afflicted I went astray, but now I keep thy statutes." As for her prayers, she said, "I have had great experience of God's hearing my Prayers, and returning comfortable Answers to me." He either granted what she prayed for, or she was satisfied without having it.

She was often perplexed that she did not feel "constant Joy" in her religious pilgrimage or the refreshing that she supposed that most of God's servants had. She was clear that he did not leave her "without the witness of his holy spirit," which she found in God's Word. Sometimes she believed that the "Gates of Hell" would never prevail against her; other times, she felt "sinkings and droopings." Feeling in the dark and seeing no way out of it, she still fell on the Lord's mercy. Satan troubled her, she believed, about the truth of the Bible, and "many times by Atheism how I could know whether there was a God." In the end, though, she had no doubts that there is a God.

Even though she was very sick and weak when she wrote all of this, she hoped that her children would have some benefit from it. She was certain that she had built her soul on the solid rock of Jesus: "I know whom I have trusted, and whom I have believed, and that he is able to keep that I have committed to his charge."

In the following poem, written August 31, 1669, Anne conveyed how tired she was and how ready she was to join her Bridegroom:

> As weary pilgrim, now at rest,
> Hugs with delight his silent nest . . .

his dangers past, and travails done . . .
A pilgrim I, on earth, perplexed
    with sins, with cares and sorrows vexed
By age and pains brought to decay
    and my Clay house mouldering away. . . .
No fainting fits shall me assail
    nor grinding pains my body frail. . . .
A Corrupt Carcass down it lies
    a glorious body it shall rise. . . .
Lord make me ready for that day
    then Come, dear bridegroom, Come away.[20]

SAILING TOWARD PORT

The young couple who sailed from England on the *Arbella* in 1630 left their indelible marks on the New World, Simon in government, Anne in poetry, and together in their many remarkable descendants, including poets, preachers, teachers, lawyers, writers, and physicians. A few distinguished descendants of the Bradstreets are these men: Richard Henry Dana Sr., essayist, editor, book reviewer, and writer of short stories, championed the Romantic poets William Wordsworth and Samuel Taylor Coleridge; Richard Henry Dana Jr. wrote *Two Years Before the Mast*, but as a lawyer, he supported abolition and served as U.S. counsel in the trial of Confederate president Jefferson Davis for treason; William Ellery Channing was a Unitarian theologian; and Wendell Phillips was an abolitionist and orator.

Poet, social critic, editor, and Harvard language professor James Russell Lowell wrote in the late nineteenth century that the Massachusetts Bay Colony was "without a parallel. It was established by a commercial company, whose members combined in themselves the two by no means incongruous elements

of religious enthusiasm and business sagacity, the earthy ingre-
dient, as in dynamite, holding in check its explosive partner,
which yet could and did explode on sufficient concussion."
Simon Bradstreet and Thomas Dudley and the other founders
truly believed that "nothing could be long profitable for the
body wherein the soul found not also her advantage."[1]

Lowell took on the critics of those founders by saying,

> The men who gave every man a chance to become a land-
> holder, who made the transfer of land easy, and put knowledge
> within the reach of all, have been called narrow-minded,
> because they were intolerant. But intolerant of what? Of
> what they believed to be dangerous nonsense, which if left
> free would destroy the last hope of civil and religious free-
> dom. They had not come here that every man might do good
> in his own eyes, but in the sight of God. Toleration, more-
> over, is something which is won, not granted.[2]

Professor Jane Eberwein offered her view of Anne's
work and the Puritan influence: "The American quality of
Bradstreet's work lies in something more subtle than imagery or choice of subject matter. It is her sensitive recording
of the Puritan people who colonized New England, with their
values, their psychology, their blind spots, and their distinc-
tive insights."[3] *Encyclopedia Britannica* profiles Anne as one of
three hundred women who changed the world, and a stained
glass window in St. Botolph's Church, Boston, in Lincolnshire,
England, honors her by depicting her in Puritan dress.

One of Anne's descendants was Oliver Wendell Holmes

Jr., chief justice of the Supreme Court of Massachusetts before he became a U.S. Supreme Court justice. He called Anne "that pale passion flower of our first spring."[4] She might have been of weak physical constitution, but her mental constitution was strong and sure. She took to heart the instruction given by her father to John Woodbridge about his serving God "in such a way whereto he had best filled him by nature, education or gifts, or graces required"[5] and applied it to herself. Both parents influenced her, but her father's support of her intellectual accomplishments cannot be overstated.

The father of Holmes Jr. and author of *The Autocrat of the Breakfast Table*, physician Oliver Wendell Holmes Sr. encouraged his readers: "To reach the port of heaven, we must sail sometimes with the wind and sometimes against it,—but we must sail, and not drift, nor lie at anchor."[6] Anne Bradstreet kept moving and kept sailing with her eyes set on the port of heaven. She was not content to lie at anchor. She asked herself what she could give to her Savior who had died for her, and she wrote this answer: "I'll serve him here whilst I shall live, / And Love him to Eternity."[7]

And she did.

NOTES

Author's Note: Anne's poems included in this book come from the 1678 edition, which was the second edition and printed in Boston. They are found in *The Works of Anne Bradstreet in Prose and Verse*, ed. John Harvard Ellis (Charlestown, MA: Abram E. Cutter, 1867). The prose was first published in Ellis's *Works*. Anne wrote her prose in a manuscript book, and her family preserved it. I have modernized some spellings when the words were unclear to present-day readers, but I have retained the punctuation. Hereafter it is cited as *Works*.

INTRODUCTION

1. John Winthrop, *The History of New England from 1630 to 1649*, notes by James Savage (Boston: Little, Brown, 1853), 29.
2. *Works*, 5.
3. Ibid., 8.
4. Ibid., 357–62.
5. Samuel Eliot Morison, *Builders of the Bay Colony* (1930, reprint, Boston: Northeastern University Press, 1981), 320.
6. Conrad Aiken, *Selected Poems* (Oxford: Oxford University Press, 1961), xiii.
7. Quoted in Jeannine Hensley, ed., *The Works of Anne Bradstreet* (Cambridge, MA: Belknap Press, 1967), xix–xx.
8. Morison, *Builders of the Bay Colony*, 335–36.
9. Library of Congress, American Treasures of the Library of Congress Imagination, http://www.loc.gov/exhibits/treasures/tri110.html.

CHAPTER 1: ENGLAND

1. Augustine Jones, *The Life and Work of Thomas Dudley: The Second Governor of Massachusetts* (Boston: Houghton, Mifflin, 1900), 25; hereafter cited as *Thomas Dudley*.

2. Mary Talcott, "The Maternal Ancestry of Governor Thomas Dudley," *New England Historical and Genealogical Register* 66 (1912): 342–43.

3. John Nichols, *The Progresses and Public Processions of Queen Elizabeth*, vol. 1 (London: John Nichols, 1823), 49.

4. Alexander Young, *Chronicles of the First Planters of the Colony of Massachusetts Bay, 1623–36* (Boston: Little and Brown, 1846), 304.

5. It is also spelled Nichols and Nicolls in sources.

6. *Thomas Dudley*, 27.

7. Ibid., 40.

8. Their dates of birth were Patience, 1616; Sarah, 1620; and Mercy, 1621.

9. Historic Church Documents, http://www.reformed.org/documents; http://www.genevabible.org.

10. 1560 Geneva Bible facsimile, http://www.greatsite.com/facsimile-reproductions/Geneva-1560-detail4.html.

11. *Thomas Dudley*, 42.

12. *Works*, 4.

13. *Thomas Dudley*, 23–24, 31.

14. Ibid., 23–24, 31–32.

15. Samuel Eliot Morison, *Builders of the Bay Colony* (Boston: Northeastern University Press, 1981, reprint) 54–55.

16. Ibid., 57.

17. Eric Foner and John A. Garraty, eds., "Puritanism," in *The Reader's Companion to American History* (Boston: Houghton Mifflin, 1991), 891.

18. John Cotton, "God's Promise to His Plantation" (1630), ed. Reiner Smolinski, 1; found at http://digitalcommons.unl.edu/etas/22 (Libraries at University of Nebraska-Lincoln); Thomas Gamble, *Data Concerning the Families of Bancroft, Bradstreet, Brown, Dudley . . . in England and America, 1277 to 1906 AD* (Savannah, GA: n.p., 1906), 43.

19. The fourth Earl of Lincoln became Speaker of the House of Lords in 1647. See http://www.thepeerage.com/p5396.htm.

20. *Works*, 4.

21. Ibid., 12–13.

22. See David Koplow, *Smallpox: The Fight to Eradicate a Global Scourge*, http://ucpress.edu/books/pages/9968.9968.ch01.php.

23. John Woodbridge, "To my dear Sister, the Author of these Poems," in *Works*, 5, 86–88.

24. *Works*, 4.

25. Ibid.

26. Isaac Greenwood, *Remarks on the Maverick Family and the Ancestry of Gov. Simon Bradstreet* (Boston: D. Clapp & Son, 1894), 1–9. Simon had two brothers: Samuel and John; a sister, Mercy, died young.

27. Helen Campbell, *Anne Bradstreet and Her Time* (Boston: D. Lothrop, 1891), chap. 2.

28. Alastair Bellany and Andrew McRae, eds., "Early Stuart Libels," *Early Modern Literary Studies* 1 (2005); see http://purl.oclc.org/emls/texts/libels.

Chapter 2: An Unexpected New Venture

1. Alice Morse Earle, *Margaret Winthrop* (New York: Charles Scribner's Sons, 1895), 115.

2. Samuel Eliot Morison, *Builders of the Bay Colony* (Boston: Northeastern University Press, 1981, reprint) 56.

3. Packer's quotations are taken from Leland Ryken's *The Puritans as They Really Were* (Grand Rapids: Zondervan, 1990), ix–xv; see also Morison, *Builders of the Bay Colony*, 58.

4. John Fiske, *The Beginnings of New England* (Boston: Houghton, Mifflin, 1898), 57–58.

5. *Thomas Dudley*, 47–48.

6. Morison, *Builders of the Bay Colony*, 52, reporting Havelock Ellis's *A Study of British Genius* (London: Hurst and Blackett, 1904).

7. Fiske, *Beginnings of New England*, 154.

8. Earle, *Margaret Winthrop*, 200; citing John R. Green, *History of the English People*, vol. 3 (London: Macmillan, 1879).

9. Alexander Young, *Chronicles of the First Planters of the Colony of Massachusetts Bay, 1623–36* (Boston: Little & Brown, 1846), 310, Thomas Dudley's words.

10. Jones, *Thomas Dudley*, 44, 46.

11. Morison, *Builders of the Bay Colony*, 53.

12. Ibid., 64. John Winthrop's *History of New England from 1630 to*

1649 provides valuable, first-person insights into the colony's founding and growth.

13. Young, *Chronicles of the First Planters*, 309.

14. Fiske, *Beginnings of New England*, 160.

CHAPTER 3: "WE SHALL BE AS A CITY UPON A HILL"

1. Robert Charles Winthrop, *Life and Letters of John Winthrop*, vol. 2 (Boston: Little, Brown, 1869), 4–5.

2. *Thomas Dudley*, 58.

3. Ibid., 46, 60.

4. Cotton, "God's Promise to His Plantation," 2.

5. Ibid., 12–14, 16–18.

6. Ibid., 18–19.

7. Ibid., 20.

8. The summary of events on the voyage from this point in the chapter until the end of Winthrop's sermon is based on Winthrop, *History of New England*, 1–29. He even included weather conditions for each day.

9. Horace E. Ware, "An Incident in Winthrop's Voyage to New England," in *Transactions for 1908–1909*, vol. 12 (Boston: Colonial Society of Massachusetts, 1911), 101.

10. George Francis Dow, *Every Day Life in the Massachusetts Bay Colony* (New York: Dover Publications, 1988), 9.

11. Stephen Mansfield, *The Search for God and Guinness* (Nashville: Thomas Nelson, 2009), 7.

12. Samuel Eliot Morison, *Builders of the Bay Colony* (Boston: Northeastern University Press, 1981 reprint), 77; Winthrop, *History of New England*, 21.

13. Frederick Weis, *The Colonial Clergy and the Colonial Churches of New England* (Lancaster, MA: n.p., 1936), 74.

14. See John Winthrop's "A Modell of Christian Charity," in Collections of the Massachusetts Historical Society, 3rd series (Boston, 1838), 7:31–48. I have modernized the spellings in the original source. It is found at http://history.hanover.edu/text/winthmod.html.

15. Morison, *Builders of the Bay Colony*, 78; June 12, cited in John Winthrop, *History of New England*, xvi.

16. *Works*, xiv.

CHAPTER 4: NEW ENGLAND

1. Robert Charles Winthrop, *Life and Letters of John Winthrop* (Boston: Little, Brown, 1869), 2:21–22.

2. Samuel Eliot Morison, *Builders of the Bay Colony* (Boston: Northeastern University Press, 1981 rept.), 78.

3. For much of what we know of their activities in the first months in New England, we have to rely on the writings of Thomas Dudley and John Winthrop. Years later Cotton Mather compiled information about this time in his *Magnalia Christi Americana*. Deputy Governor Dudley's Letter to the Countess of Lincoln appears in Young, *Chronicles of the First Planters*, 301–42.

4. Morison, *Builders of the Bay Colony*, 78.

5. *Thomas Dudley*, 77.

6. Ibid., 79.

7. Charlotte Gordon, *Mistress Bradstreet: The Untold Life of America's First Poet* (New York: Little, Brown, 2005), 10–11.

8. Alexander Young, *Chronicles of the First Planters of the Colony of Massachusetts Bay, 1623–36* (Boston: Little & Brown, 1846), 312–13.

9. Morison, *Builders of the Bay Colony*, 136.

10. Ibid., 80–81.

11. Jones, *Thomas Dudley*, 80–81.

12. Ibid.

13. Leland Ryken, *The Puritans as They Really Were* (Grand Rapids: Zondervan, 1990), 112, 118.

14. *Works*, xxl, xv; see http://www.firstchurchboston.org/events/category; http://www.masshist.org/findingaids/doc.cfm?fa=fa0030; Gordon, *Mistress Bradstreet*, 112.

15. See http://www.masshist.org/findingaids/doc.cfm?fa=fa0030.

16. *Thomas Dudley*, 81; Gamble, *Data Concerning the Families*, 4d.

17. *Thomas Dudley*, 91.

18. *Works*, 16.

19. Young, *Chronicles of the First Planters*, 325.

20. Charles Henry Browning, *Americans of Royal Descent* (Philadelphia: Porter & Coates, 1891), 482.

21. *Thomas Dudley*, 46.

22. Morison, *Builders of the Bay Colony*, 80.

23. Alice Morse Earle, *Customs and Fashions in Old New England* (New York: Charles Scribner's Sons, 1893), 147.

24. Ibid., 148–49.

25. Michael Sletcher, ed., *New England* (Westport, CT: Greenwood Press, 2004), 237–38.

26. Winthrop, *Life and Letters*, 2:38.

27. Young, *Chronicles of the First Planters*, 319; Morison, *Builders of the Bay Colony*, 78.

28. Morison, *Builders of the Bay Colony*, October 19, 85; http://www.mayflowerfamilies.com/important_names_events/mass_bay_colony_freemen_1630.htm.

29. Young, *Chronicles of the First Planters*, 321; Walter Blair et al., *The Literature of the United States*, 3rd ed., vol. 1 (Glenview, IL: Scott, Foresman, 1971), 68–69.

30. Morison, *Builders of the Bay Colony*, 82.

31. Young, *Chronicles of the First Planters*, 330–32.

32. Jim Vrabel, *When in Boston* (Boston: Northeastern University Press, 2004), 8.

33. *Thomas Dudley*, 98, 105; Massachusetts Bay Colony marker, http://freepages.genealogy.rootsweb.ancestry.com.

34. *Thomas Dudley*, 125; Winthrop, *Life and Letters*, 2:95.

35. Mary Crawford, *Social Life in Old New England* (Boston: Little, Brown, 1914), 240–41.

36. *Thomas Dudley*, 100.

37. *Works*, 365.

38. Eve LaPlante, *American Jezebel* (San Francisco: HarperSanFrancisco, 2004), 72–74.

Chapter 5: A Home at Last

1. Alexander Young, *Chronicles of the First Planters of the First Colony of Massachusetts Bay, 1623–36* (Boston: Little & Brown, 1846), 305.

2. *Works*, xxxiii; Poets of Cambridge, U.S.A., Anne Bradstreet, http://www.harvardsquarelibrary.org/poets/bradstreet.php; historic markers, Cambridge, MA, http://www.cambridgema.gov/~Historic/markers.html#stations; *Thomas Dudley*, 124.

3. Robert Charles Winthrop, *Life and Letters of John Winthrop* (Boston: Little, Brown, 1869), 2:94.

4. Samuel Eliot Morison, *Builders of the Bay Colony* (Boston: Northeastern University Press, 1981 reprint), 76.

5. Alice Morse Earle, *Customs and Fashions in Old New England* (New York: Charles Scribner's Sons, 1893), 108, 121, 126.

6. Young, *Chronicles of the First Planters*, 324.

7. Leland Ryken, *The Puritans as They Really Were* (Grand Rapids: Zondervan, 1990), 20, 25, 32.

8. Wood is quoted in Young's *Chronicles of the First Planters*, 413.

9. *Thomas Dudley*, 123.

10. Young, *Chronicles of the First Planters*, 397, 399.

11. Alice Morse Earle, *Margaret Winthrop* (New York: Charles Scribner's Sons, 1895), 183–84.

12. Ibid., 195–97; Mary Crawford, *Social Life in Old New England* (Boston: Little, Brown, 1914), 241.

13. Crawford, *Social Life in Old New England*, 202.

14. *Thomas Dudley*, 467.

15. Earle, *Margaret Winthrop*, 261.

16. *Works*, 5, 391–92.

CHAPTER 6: "IT PLEASED GOD"

1. *Works*, 5.

2. Richard W. Wertz and Dorothy C. Wertz, *Lying-in: A History of Childbirth in America*, expanded ed. (New Haven, CT: Yale University Press: 1989), 1–5, 19–20.

3. *Works*, 50, Meditation 10.

4. See http://www.1911Encyclopedia.org/William_Prynne; http://www.british-civil-wars.co.uk/biog/prynne.htm.

5. Samuel Eliot Morison, *Builders of the Bay Colony* (Boston: Northeastern University Press, 1981, reprint), 130.

6. Mary Crawford, *Social Life in Old New England* (Boston: Little, Brown, 1914), 147–49.

7. *Thomas Dudley*, 269.

8. John Fiske, *The Beginnings of New England* (Boston: Houghton, Mifflin, 1898), 163–64.

9. Richard Hofstadter, *Anti-Intellectualism in American Life* (New York: Knopf, 1963), 59.

10. Leland Ryken, *The Puritans as They Really Were* (Grand Rapids: Zondervan, 1990), 128.

11. Crawford, *Social Life in Old New England*, 147–49.
12. *Thomas Dudley*, 154.
13. John Cotton, "Catechism," in Gerald Garth Johnson, *Puritan Children in Exile* (Bowie, MD: Heritage Books, 2002), 195–220; it was printed in 1646 in England, see http://digitalcommons.unl.edu/etas/18 (Libraries at University of Nebraska-Lincoln).
14. *Works*, 381–85.
15. Ibid.
16. Mencken cited in Ryken, *The Puritans as They Really Were*, 1.
17. Samuel Eliot Morison, *Builders of the Bay Colony* (Boston: Northeastern University Press, 1981 reprint), 135; Ryken, *The Puritans as They Really Were*, 2.
18. Derek Vaillant, *Sounds of Reform: Progressivism and Music in Chicago, 1873–1935* (Chapel Hill: University of North Carolina Press, 2003), 188.
19. Morison, *Builders of the Bay Colony*, 289.
20. Alice Morse Earle, *Customs and Fashions in Old New England* (New York: Charles Scribner's Sons, 1893), 316–17.
21. Ibid.
22. See http://www.history.army/mil/Reference/mamil/Mamil.htm; Nelson Manfred Blake, *A History of American Life and Thought* (New York: McGraw-Hill, 1963), 66.
23. *Thomas Dudley*, 124.
24. Ibid., 181–82.
25. Gamble, *Data Concerning the Families*, 9d.
26. Oliver Ayer Roberts, *History of the Military Company of the Massachusetts*, vol. 1 (Boston: Mudge and Son, 1895), 104; Alonzo Lewis, *The History of Lynn*, 2d. ed. (Boston: Samuel Dickinson, 1844), 116–17; Martha Saxton, *Being Good: Women's Moral Values in Early America* (New York: Farrar, Straus and Giroux, 2003), 33–34; James R. Newhall, *The Great and General Courte in Colonie Times* (Lynn, MA: Nichols Press, 1897), 51–97.
27. Marker, http://freepages.genealogy.rootsweb.ancestry.com.
28. Morison, *Builders of the Bay Colony*, 223; *Thomas Dudley*, 105.

CHAPTER 7: IN THE WILDERNESS

1. Gamble, *Data Concerning the Families*, 59.

2. Samuel Eliot Morison, *Builders of the Bay Colony* (Boston: Northeastern University Press, 1981 reprint), 271.

3. Thomas Franklin Waters, *The Development of Our Town Government and Common Lands and Commonage* (Salem, MA: Salem Press, 1900), 23.

4. Ipswich Historical Society, *Thomas Dudley and Simon and Ann Bradstreet: A Study of House-Lots* (Salem, MA: Salem Press, 1903), 12, 45; Morison, *Builders of the Bay Colony*, 223.

5. Waters, *Development of Our Town Government*, 5.

6. Biography, John Winthrop Jr., Connecticut State Library, http://www.cslibrary.org/winthropj.htm.

7. *Thomas Dudley*, 211.

8. Alden T. Vaughan, *New England Frontier: Puritans and Indians, 1620–1675*, 3rd ed. (Norman: University of Oklahoma Press, 1995), 104, 187.

9. Ipswich Historical Society, *Dudley and Bradstreet*, 20.

10. Thomas Franklin Waters, *The Meeting House Green and a Study of Houses and Lands in That Vicinity* (Salem, MA: Salem Press, 1902), 5, 10.

11. For a chronology of the Pequot War, see http://bc.barnard.columbia.edu/~rmccaugh/earlyAC/pequottl.htm.

12. Vaughan, *New England Frontier*, xxiv–xxv.

13. Ibid., 107, 197, 201.

14. Ibid., 195, 336.

15. Morison, *Builders of the Bay Colony*, 272.

16. Alice Morse Earle, *Margaret Winthrop* (New York: Charles Scribner's Sons, 1895), 183–84.

17. Jones, *Thomas Dudley*, 212.

18. Ibid., 421.

19. *Records and Files of the Quarterly Courts of Essex County, Massachusetts*, vol. 3, 1662–1667 (Salem: Essex Institute, 1913), 47.

20. Leland Ryken, *The Puritans as They Really Were* (Grand Rapids: Zondervan, 1990), 39; Richard Godbeer, *Sexual Revolution in Early America* (Baltimore: Johns Hopkins University Press, 2002), 59.

21. See Helen Campbell, *Anne Bradstreet and Her Time* (Boston: D. Lothrop, 1891), chap. 5, for more about Simon and Anne's relationship.

22. *Works*, 394.

23. Ibid., 393.

24. Ibid., 394–95.

25. Ibid., 395–98.

26. Morison, *Builders of the Bay Colony*, 183.

27. Samuel Eliot Morison, *The Oxford History of the American People*, vol. 1 (New York: New American Library, 1972), 114; *Thomas Dudley*, 287.

28. Nelson Manfred Blake, *A History of American Life and Thought* (New York: McGraw-Hill, 1963), 56.

29. Morison, *Builders of the Bay Colony*, 189; Morison, *The Oxford History of the American People*, 1:114; Harvard Guide, http://www.news.harvard.edu/guide/intro/index.html.

30. *Works*, 370–81.

31. Robert D. Richardson Jr., "The Puritan Poetry of Anne Bradstreet," in *The American Puritan Imagination*, ed. Sacvan Bercovitch (London: Cambridge University Press, 1974), 114.

Chapter 8: Mistress Hutchinson

1. Thomas Shepard's *Memoir of His Own Life*, in Alexander Young, *Chronicles of the First Planters of the Colony of Massachusetts Bay 1623–36* (Boston: Little & Brown, 1846), 499, 517, 556–58.

2. Francis J. Bremer, ed., *Anne Hutchinson: Troubler of the Puritan Zion* (Huntington, NY: Krieger, 1981), 1.

3. Charles F. Adams, *Three Episodes of Massachusetts History: The Settlement of Boston*, vol. 1 (Boston: Houghton, Mifflin, 1892), 394–95, 397, 402.

4. Eve LaPlante, *American Jezebel* (San Francisco: HarperSanFrancisco, 2004), 7.

5. Adams, *Three Episodes of Massachusetts History*, 1:381.

6. Winnifred King Rugg, *Unafraid: A Life of Anne Hutchinson* (Boston: Houghton Mifflin, 1930), 100.

7. Samuel Eliot Morison, *The Founding of Harvard College* (Cambridge, MA: Harvard University Press, 1935), 178.

8. See http://www.scribd.com/doc/12946/Transcript-of-Anne-Hutchinson-Trial.

9. Jacob Bailey Moore, *Memoirs of American Governors*, vol. 1 (New York: Gates & Stedman, 1846), 48–49.

10. Morison, *Founding of Harvard College*, 178.

11. Ibid.

12. Wendy Martin, *An American Triptych: Anne Bradstreet, Emily Dickinson, Adrienne Rich* (Chapel Hill: University of North Carolina Press, 1984), 64, citing Winthrop, *Short Story of the Rise, Reign, and Ruin of the Antinomians, Familists, and Libertines*, 14.

13. See http://massmoments.org/moment.cfm?mid=88.

Chapter 9: Liberties and Losses

1. Samuel Eliot Morison, *Builders of the Bay Colony* (Boston: Northeastern University Press, 1981 reprint), 333, 335–36.

2. See Health in the 17th Century (specifically in England), www.nmm.ac.uk/places/queens-house/fact-files/health-in-the-17th-century.

3. John Ballard Blake, *Public Health in the Town of Boston, 1630–1822* (Cambridge: Harvard University Press, 1959), 2–3; www.mayflowerfamilies.com/colonial_life/colonial_diseases.htm.

4. John Josselyn, *New-England's Rarities* (Boston: William Veazie, 1865), 96, 115; Josselyn's first trip to New England took place in 1638.

5. Alice Morse Earle, *Customs and Fashions in Old New England* (New York: Charles Scribner's Sons, 1893), 246–48; Michael McCarthy, "Granny Was Right: Herbal Remedies Can Help Speed Healing Process," *Independent* (U.K.), July 14, 2001; Nicholas Culpeper, *Culpeper's Complete Herbal* (1653; reprint, London: Thomas Kelly, 1835), 39, 41, 53, 61, 136.

6. *Compendium of Physick*, 1671, in Zerobabel Endecott, *Synopsis Medicinae* (Salem: n.p., 1914), 16.

7. Culpeper, *Culpeper's Complete Herbal*, 53, 136.

8. Endecott, *Synopsis Medicinae*, 20, difficult labor.

9. Josselyn, *New-England's Rarities*, 141–47.

10. Charles McLean Andrews, *Colonial Folkways* (New Haven: Yale University Press, 1919), 97, 99, 101.

11. William Grimes, *Straight Up or on the Rocks* (New York: North Point Press, 2001), 16–20.

12. James M. Volo and Dorothy D. Volo, *Family Life in 17th- and*

18th-Century America (Westport, CT: Greenwood Press, 2006), 209–11.

13. Earle, *Customs and Fashions in Old New England*, 133–36.

14. (London: printed for John Browne, 1615); http://www.uni-giessen.de/gloning/tx/1615murr.htm.

15. Ibid.

16. Volo and Volo, *Family Life*, 208, 211–15, 230–32.

17. Elizabeth Ferszt, "Transatlantic Dame School?: Anne Bradstreet's Early Poems as Pedagogy" (Ph.D. diss., Ferris State University, 24 January, 2008).

18. *Works*, 345–52.

19. See act 4, scene 1, line 91; the usage dates to 1570, according to the 2010 *Random House Unabridged Dictionary*.

20. *Thomas Dudley*, 259–60.

21. Ibid.

22. See www.oldsouth.org/pubs/BayPsalmBook/BayPsalmBook.html.

23. John Fiske, *The Beginnings of New England* (Boston: Houghton, Mifflin, 1898), 137.

24. Morison, *Builders of the Bay Colony*, 219; Francis Bremer, *The Puritan Experiment: New England Society from Bradford to Edwards* (Lebanon, NH: University Press of New England, 1995), 62.

25. See http://history.hanover.edu/texts/masslib.html; Morison, *Builders of the Bay Colony*, 232, 234. The information in this paragraph and the following two paragraphs is from these sources.

26. *Colonial Origins of the American Constitutions*, ed. Donald S. Lutz (Indianapolis: Liberty Fund, 1998); Richard Quinney, *The Social Reality of Crime* (New Brunswick, NJ: Transaction Publishers, 2008), 62–63. Information from this paragraph and the next paragraph is from these sources.

27. *Works*, 330–43.

28. Ibid.

29. *Thomas Dudley*, 295, 297–98.

30. George Ballard, *Memoirs of Several Ladies of Great Britain* (Oxford: W. Jackson, 1752), 211–21.

31. *Works*, 357–62.

32. Ibid., 369.

CHAPTER 10: ANDOVER

1. *Thomas Dudley*, 320.
2. See http://www.ipswichma.com/directory/history.asp for more information about Andover in its early days.
3. *Thomas Dudley*, 287.
4. Gamble, *Data Concerning the Families*, 48; Ipswich Historical Society, *Dudley and Bradstreet*, 29.
5. Samuel Eliot Morison, *Builders of the Bay Colony* (Boston: Northeastern University Press, 1981 reprint), 143, 145, 155.
6. Samuel Eliot Morison, *The Oxford History of the American People* (New York: New American Library, 1972), 1:113.
7. *Works*, 53, Meditation 23.
8. Morison, *The Oxford History of the American People*, 1:114; Blake, *A History of American Life and Thought*, 57.
9. Helen Campbell, *Anne Bradstreet and Her Time* (Boston: D. Lothrop, 1891), see latter part of chap. 10 for more about Andover.
10. The story of Sarah's plight comes from *Thomas Dudley*, 469–71; see also Laurel Thatcher Ulrich, *Good Wives: Image and Reality in the Lives of Women in Northern New England* (New York: Vintage, 1991), 112.
11. Ibid.
12. Ibid.
13. Blake, *A History of American Life and Thought*, 64.
14. Roberts, *History of the Military Company of the Massachusetts*, 1:68.
15. *Thomas Dudley*, 469–71.
16. Ibid., 199.
17. Ibid., 468; Louis Mitchell et al., eds., *Woodbridge Record: Being an Account of the Descendants of the Rev. John Woodbridge* (New Haven: n.p., 1883), 6.

CHAPTER 11: *THE TENTH MUSE LATELY SPRUNG UP IN AMERICA*

1. *Works*, 84.
2. Nathaniel Ward, *The Simple Cobler of Aggawam in America* (1647; reprint, Salem, MA: Salem Press, 1905), 26–27.

3. *Works*, 83–84.

4. Ibid., 89.

5. Ibid., 93–96.

6. Luther Caldwell cited in Gamble, *Data Concerning the Families*, 58a.

7. *Works*, 100–102.

8. Charles Wells Moulton, *The Library of Literary Criticism of English and American Authors, 1639–1729*, vol. 2 (Buffalo: Moulton Publishing, 1901), citing James Anderson, *Memorable Women of Puritan Times* (1861), 1:174.

9. All quotations from the poems in this chapter are from *Works* 103–21, 123–41, 147–67, 168–80, 181–324, 398–99, 353–56, 363–64, 386–88.

10. George Ballard, *Memoirs of Several Ladies of Great Britain* (Oxford: W. Jackson, 1752), 251.

11. Gordon, *Mistress Bradstreet*, 253.

12. *Winthrop's Journal: History of New England*, ed. James Kendall Hosmer (New York: Charles Scribner's Sons, 1908), 2:225, April 13, 1645.

13. Susan Wiseman, *Conspiracy and Virtue: Women, Writing, and Politics in Seventeenth-Century England* (New York: Oxford University Press, 2006), 199–200, 202.

14. Phyllis Mack, *Visionary Women: Ecstatic Prophecy in Seventeenth-Century England* (Berkeley, CA: University of California Press, 1992), 92–93; John James Currier, *History of Newbury, Mass., 1635–1902*, vol. 1 (Boston: Damrell & Upham, 1902), 324.

15. See http://www.english.cam.ac.uk/wroth/biography.htm.

16. Hugh James Rose, *A New General Biographical Dictionary* (London: n.p., 1857).

17. Ballard, *Memoirs of Several Ladies of Great Britain*, 337–45.

18. Cotton Mather, *Magnalia Christi Americana*, vol. 1 (Hartford: Silas Andrus and Son, 1855), 135.

CHAPTER 12: LAMENTATIONS

1. *Thomas Dudley*, 382.

2. Collections of the Massachusetts Historical Society, vol. 7 (Boston: Massachusetts Historical Society, 1865), 255.

3. *Thomas Dudley*, 403–4; Collections of the Massachusetts Historical Society, vol. 2 (Boston: Massachusetts Historical Society, 1854), 117.

4. *Works*, 365–67.

5. Gamble, *Data Concerning the Families*, 10d.

6. *Thomas Dudley*, 417–22.

7. Ibid.

8. *Works*, 16–17, July 8, 1656.

9. Ibid., 20.

10. Ibid., 21.

11. Ibid., 22, May 13.

12. Ibid., 23–24, September 30, 1657.

13. Perry Miller and Thomas Johnson, eds., *The Puritans: A Sourcebook of Their Writings* (Toronto: General Publishing, 2001), 631.

14. *Works*, 24.

15. Ibid., 400–403.

16. Eve LaPlante, *American Jezebel* (San Francisco: HarperSanFrancisco, 2004), 225.

17. George Edward Ellis, *Puritan Age and Rule in the Colony of the Massachusetts Bay, 1629–1685* (New York: Ben Franklin, 1970), 409–44.

18. Bishop is quoted in Sarah Loring Bailey, *Historical Sketches of Andover* (Boston: Houghton, Mifflin, 1880), 414–15.

19. Ibid.

20. LaPlante, *American Jezebel*, 253–54.

CHAPTER 13: "WEARY PILGRIM, NOW AT REST"

1. John Richard Green, *History of the English People*, 3:328.

2. *Works*, 25.

3. Ibid., 27.

4. Ibid., 28.; both the poem and the information about Hannah's marriage come from this page.

5. Ibid.

6. Gamble, *Data Concerning the Families*, 51.

7. *Works*, 32–33.

8. Ibid., 34–37.

9. Ibid., 38–39.

10. Gamble, *Data Concerning the Families*, 51; Ellis, *Puritan Age and Rule*, 500, 504; *Works*, 32n.

11. Sarah Loring Bailey, *Historical Sketches of Andover* (Boston: Houghton Mifflin, 1880), 127, 129.

12. *Works*, 40–42.

13. Ibid., 389–90.

14. Ibid., 328–29.

15. Ibid., 404–406. Lines about the deaths of her grandchildren and daughter-in-law and the information about Simon Bradstreet's will are from these pages.

16. Information in this paragraph comes from James Anderson, *Memorable Women of the Puritan Times* (Whitefish, MT: Kessinger, 2003), 177.

17. *Works*, 409–13.

18. Ibid., 4, 48–73.

19. Anne's comments to her children from this point up to the final poem in this chapter are from *Works*, 3–10.

20. Ibid., 42–43.

CHAPTER 14: SAILING TOWARD PORT

1. James Russell Lowell, *The Writings of James Russell Lowell: Literary and Political Addresses* (Cambridge: Riverside Press, 1890), 146.

2. James Russell Lowell, *Among My Books* (Boston: Houghton Mifflin, 1888), 242.

3. Jane D. Eberwein, ed., *Early American Poetry: Selections from Bradstreet, Taylor, Dwight, Freneau, and Bryant* (Madison: University of Wisconsin Press, 1978), 8.

4. Ipswich Historical Society, *Dudley and Bradstreet*, 34.

5. *Thomas Dudley*, 287.

6. Oliver Wendell Holmes Sr., *The Autocrat of the Breakfast Table* (1858; reprint, Boston: Houghton, Mifflin, 1894), 136.

7. *Works*, Meditation 4, 11.

SELECTED
BIBLIOGRAPHY

Books listed here were consulted in the writing of this book, providing background information on the historical period as well as information specific to Anne Bradstreet, her family, her works, and her times.

Adams, Charles F. *Three Episodes of Massachusetts History: The Settlement of Boston*. Vol. 1. Boston: Houghton, Mifflin, 1892.

Anderson, James. *Memorable Women of the Puritan Times*. Whitefish, MT: Kessinger, 2003.

Anderson, Robert Charles. *Great Migration Begins: Immigrants to New England, 1620–33*. 3 vols. Boston: New England Historic Genealogical Society, 1995.

Andrews, Charles McLean. *Colonial Folkways*. New Haven: Yale University Press, 1919.

Bailey, Sarah Loring. *Historical Sketches of Andover*. Boston: Houghton, Mifflin, 1880.

Ballard, George. *Memoirs of Several Ladies of Great Britain*. Oxford: W. Jackson, 1752.

Blair, Walter, et al. *The Literature of the United States*. 3rd ed. Vol. 1. Glenview, IL: Scott, Foresman, 1971.

Blake, John Ballard. *Public Health in the Town of Boston, 1630–1822*. Cambridge: Harvard University Press, 1959.

Blake, Nelson Manfred. *A History of American Life and Thought*. New York: McGraw-Hill, 1963.

Bradstreet, Anne. *The Works of Anne Bradstreet*. Edited by Jeannine Hensley. Cambridge, MA: Belknap Press, 1967.

Bremer, Francis J., ed. *Anne Hutchinson: Troubler of the Puritan Zion*. Huntington, NY: Krieger, 1981.

Bremer, Francis. *The Puritan Experiment: New England Society from Bradford to Edwards*. Lebanon, NH: University Press of New England, 1995.

Caldwell, Luther, ed. *An Account of Anne Bradstreet: The Puritan Poetess*. Boston: Damrell & Upham, 1898.

Campbell, Helen. *Anne Bradstreet and Her Time*. Boston: D. Lothrop, 1891.

Collections of the Massachusetts Historical Society. Vol. 7. Boston: Massachusetts Historical Society, 1865.

Compendium of Physick, 1671. In Zerobabel Endecott's *Synopsis Medicinae*. Salem: n.p., 1914.

Cotton, John. "God's Promise to His Plantation" (1630). Edited by Reiner Smolinski. See http://digitalcommons.unl.edu/etas/22 (Libraries at University of Nebraska-Lincoln).

Crawford, Mary. *Social Life in Old New England*. Boston: Little, Brown, 1914.

Culpeper, Nicholas. *Culpeper's Complete Herbal*. 1653. Reprint, London: Thomas Kelly, 1835.

Currier, John James. *History of Newbury, Mass., 1635–1902*. Vol. 1. Boston: Damrell & Upham, 1902.

Cutter, William Richard. *New England Families*. Vol. 1. New York: Lewis Historical Publishing Co., 1914.

Daniels, Bruce C. *Puritans at Play: Leisure and Recreation in Colonial New England*. New York: St. Martin's Press, 1995.

Davis, Cynthia J., and Kathryn West. *Women Writers in the United States: A Timeline of Literary, Cultural, and Social History*. New York: Oxford University Press, 1996.

Dean, John. *Pedigree of Bradstreet*. 1800, n.p.

Dow, George Francis. *Every Day Life in the Massachusetts Bay Colony*. New York: Dover Publications, 1988.

Earle, Alice Morse. *Customs and Fashions in Old New England*. New York: Charles Scribner's Sons, 1893.

———. *Margaret Winthrop*. New York: Charles Scribner's Sons, 1895.

Eberwein, Jane Donahue, ed. *Early American Poetry: Selections from Bradstreet, Taylor, Dwight, Freneau, and Bryant.* Madison: University of Wisconsin Press, 1978.

Eberwein, Jane Donahue. "The 'Unrefined Ore' of Anne Bradstreet's Quaternions." *Early American Literature* 9 (1974): 19–24.

Ellis, George Edward. *Puritan Age and Rule in the Colony of the Massachusetts Bay, 1629–1685.* New York: Ben Franklin, 1970.

Ellis, John Harvard, ed. *The Works of Anne Bradstreet in Prose and Verse.* Charlestown, MA: Abram E. Cutter, 1867.

Ferszt, Elizabeth. "Transatlantic Dame School?: Anne Bradstreet's Early Poems as Pedagogy." PhD diss., Ferris State University, 2008.

Fiske, John. *The Beginnings of New England.* Boston: Houghton, Mifflin, 1898.

Gamble, Thomas. *Data Concerning the Families of Bancroft, Bradstreet, Brown, Dudley . . . in England and America, 1277 to 1906 AD.* Savannah, GA: n.p., 1906.

Geneva Bible, 1560 facsimile. http://www.greatsite.com/facsimile-reproductions/Geneva-1560-detail4.html.

Godbeer, Richard. *Sexual Revolution in Early America.* Baltimore: Johns Hopkins University Press, 2002.

Gordon, Charlotte. *Mistress Bradstreet: The Untold Life of America's First Poet.* New York: Little, Brown, 2005.

Greenwood, Isaac. *Remarks on the Maverick Family and the Ancestry of Gov. Simon Bradstreet.* Boston: D. Clapp & Son, 1894.

Greven, Philip J. *Four Generations: Population, Land and Family in Colonial Andover, Massachusetts.* Ithaca, NY: Cornell University, 1970.

Gribben, Crawford. *God's Irishmen: Theological Debates in Cromwellian Ireland.* New York: Oxford University Press, 2007.

Health in the 17th Century. See http://www.nmm.ac.uk/places/queens-house/fact-files/health-in-the-17th-century.

Historical Markers Erected by Massachusetts Bay Colony Tercentenary Commission. See http://www.archive.org/stream/historicalmarker-00mass/historicalmaker00mass_djvu.txt.

Holmes, Oliver Wendell, Sr. *The Autocrat of the Breakfast Table.* Boston: Houghton, Mifflin, 1894.

Hosmer, James Kendall, ed. *Winthrop's Journal: History of New England.* New York: Charles Scribner's Sons, 1908.

Ipswich Historical Society. *Thomas Dudley and Simon and Ann Bradstreet: A Study of House-Lots*. Salem, MA: Salem Press, 1903.

Johnson, Gerald Garth. *Puritan Children in Exile*. Bowie, MD: Heritage Books: 2002.

Jones, Augustine. *The Life and Work of Thomas Dudley: The Second Governor of Massachusetts*. Boston: Houghton, Mifflin, 1900.

Josselyn, John. *New-England's Rarities*. Boston: William Veazie, 1865.

LaPlante, Eve. *American Jezebel*. San Francisco: HarperSanFrancisco, 2004.

Lewis, Alonzo. *The History of Lynn*. 2nd ed. Boston: Samuel Dickinson, 1844.

Lowell, James Russell. *Among My Books*. Boston: Houghton Mifflin, 1888.

———. *The Writings of James Russell Lowell: Literary and Political Addresses*. Cambridge: Riverside Press, 1890.

Lutz, Donald S., ed. *Colonial Origins of the American Constitutions*. Indianapolis: Liberty Fund, 1998.

Mack, Phyllis. *Visionary Women: Ecstatic Prophecy in Seventeenth-Century England*. Berkeley: University of California Press, 1992.

Mansfield, Stephen. *The Search for God and Guinness*. Nashville: Thomas Nelson, 2009.

Martin, Wendy. *An American Triptych: Anne Bradstreet, Emily Dickinson, Adrienne Rich*. Chapel Hill: University of North Carolina Press, 1984.

Mather, Cotton. *Magnalia Christi Americana*. Vol. 1. Hartford: Silas Andrus and Son, 1855.

Miller, Perry, and Thomas Johnson, eds. *The Puritans: A Sourcebook of Their Writings*. Toronto: General Publishing, 2001.

Monaghan, E. Jennifer. *Learning to Read and Write in Colonial America*. Amherst: University of Massachusetts Press, 2005.

Morgan, Edmund. *Puritan Family*. New York: Harper and Row, 1983.

Morison, Samuel Eliot. *Builders of the Bay Colony*. 1930. Reprint, Boston: Northeastern University Press, 1981.

———. *The Oxford History of the American People*. Vol. 1. New York: New American Library, 1972.

Moulton, Charles Wells. *The Library of Literary Criticism of English and American Authors, 1639–1729*. Vol. 2. Buffalo: Moulton Publishing Co., 1901.

Murrell, John. *A New Book of Cookerie*. London: printed for John Browne, 1615. See http://www.uni-giessen.de/gloning/tx/1615murr.htm.

Newhall, James R. *The Great and General Courte in Colonie Times*. Lynn, MA: Nichols Press, 1897.

Phillips, Wendell. Speech, 21 Dec., 1855, in *Familiar Quotations*. Edited by John Bartlett. 10th ed. Boston: Little, Brown, 1919.

Poetry Landmark: The Search for Anne Bradstreet. See http://wwwpoets.org/viewmedia.php.prmMMID/5766.

Poets of Cambridge, U.S.A. Anne Bradstreet. See http://www.harvardsquarelibrary.org/poets/bradstreet.php.

Quinney, Richard. *The Social Reality of Crime*. New Brunswick, NJ: Transaction Publishers, 2008.

Records and Files of the Quarterly Courts of Essex County, Massachusetts. Vol. 3, 1662–1667. Salem: Essex Institute, 1913.

Richardson, Robert D., Jr. "The Puritan Poetry of Anne Bradstreet." In *The American Puritan Imagination*. Edited by Sacvan Bercovitch. London: Cambridge University Press, 1974.

Roberts, Oliver Ayer. *History of the Military Company of the Massachusetts*. Vol. 1. Boston: Mudge and Son, 1895.

Rose, Hugh James. *A New General Biographical Dictionary*. London: n.p., 1857.

Rugg, Winnifred King. *Unafraid: A Life of Anne Hutchinson*. Boston: Houghton Mifflin, 1930.

Ryken, Leland. *The Puritans as They Really Were*. Grand Rapids: Zondervan, 1990.

Saxton, Martha. *Being Good: Women's Moral Values in Early America*. New York: Farrar, Straus and Giroux, 2003.

Schlesinger, Arthur M., Jr., ed. *The Almanac of American History*. New York: Bramhall House, 1986.

Sletcher, Michael, ed. *New England*. Westport, CT: Greenwood Press, 2004.

Talcott, Mary. "The Maternal Ancestry of Governor Thomas Dudley." *New England Historical and Genealogical Register* 66 (1912): 342–43.

Trager, James. *The Women's Chronology*. New York: Henry Holt, 1994.

Ulrich, Laurel Thatcher. *Good Wives: Image and Reality in the Lives of Women in Northern New England*. New York: Vintage, 1991.

Vaillant, Derek. *Sounds of Reform: Progressivism and Music in Chicago, 1873–1935*. Chapel Hill: University of North Carolina Press, 2003.

Vaughan, Alden T. *New England Frontier: Puritans and Indians, 1620–1675*. 3rd ed. Norman: University of Oklahoma Press, 1995.

Volo, James M., and Dorothy Denneen Volo. *Family Life in 17th- and 18th-Century America*. Westport, CT: Greenwood Press, 2006.

Ward, Nathaniel. *The Simple Cobler of Aggawam in America*. 1647. Reprint, Salem, MA: Salem Press, 1905.

Waters, Thomas Franklin. *The Development of Our Town Government and Common Lands and Commonage*. Salem, MA: Salem Press, 1900.

———. *Ipswich in the Massachusetts Bay Colony*. Ipswich: Ipswich Historical Society, 1905.

———. *The Meeting House Green and a Study of Houses and Lands in That Vicinity*. Salem, MA: Salem Press, 1902.

Weis, Frederick L. *The Ancestry of Governor Thomas Dudley*. Peterborough, NH: Sims Press, 1962.

———. *The Colonial Clergy and the Colonial Churches of New England*. Lancaster, MA: n.p., 1936.

Wertz, Richard W., and Dorothy C. Wertz. *Lying-in: A History of Childbirth in America*. Expanded ed. New Haven, CT: Yale University Press, 1989.

West, Willis Mason. *The Story of American Democracy, Political and Industrial*. Boston: Small, Maynard & Company, 1922.

White, Elizabeth. *Anne Bradstreet: The Tenth Muse*. New York: Oxford University Press, 1971.

Wilson, David Harris. *A History of England*. New York: Holt, Rinehart & Winston, 1967.

Wilson, James G., et al. *Appleton's Cyclopedia of American Biography*. New York: D. Appleton and Company, 1887–89.

Winthrop, John. "A Model of Christian Charity." In Collections of the Massachusetts Historical Society, 3rd series. Boston, 1838.

———. *The History of New England from 1630 to 1649*. Notes by James Savage. Boston: Little, Brown, 1853.

Winthrop, Robert Charles. *Life and Letters of John Winthrop*. Vol. 2. Boston: Little, Brown, 1869.

Wintle, Justin, ed. *Makers of Modern Culture*. London: Routledge & Kegan Paul, 1981.

Wiseman, Susan. *Conspiracy and Virtue: Women, Writing, and Politics in Seventeenth-Century England*. New York: Oxford University Press, 2006.

Young, Alexander. *Chronicles of the First Planters of the Colony of Massachusetts Bay, 1623–36*. Boston: Little & Brown, 1846.

ABOUT THE AUTHOR

D. B. Kellogg has a passion for telling people's stories. She is the author or coauthor of several biographies, institutional histories, family histories, and the performing arts history of Nashville, Tennessee.

Close Encounters of the Christian Kind

Available Now

JANE AUSTEN
9781595553027

ANNE BRADSTREET
9781595551092

WILLIAM F. BUCKLEY
9781595550651

JOHN BUNYAN
9781595553041

WINSTON CHURCHILL
9781595553065

ISAAC NEWTON
9781595553034

SAINT FRANCIS
9781595551078

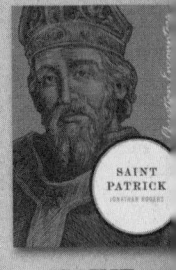

SAINT PATRICK
9781595553058

Available October 2010

D. L. MOODY
9781595550477

SAINT NICHOLAS
9781595551153

SERGEANT YORK
9781595550255